Leckie×Leckie
Scotland's leading educational publishers

Success guides

D1079519

INTERMEDIATE 2 & HIGHER
English Essay Skills
for the Writing Portfolio

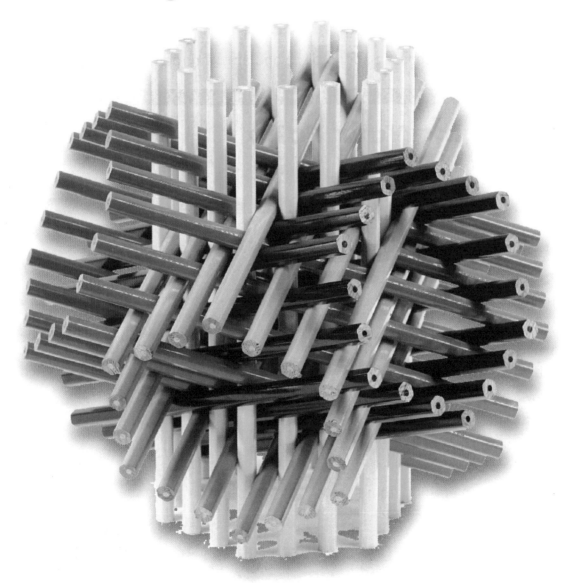

Dr Christopher Nicol

Contents

1 Introduction

Introduction 5

2 How the Folio is Assessed

How the folio is assessed 6

3 How the Folio Differs

What's the difference between a folio piece and an exam room essay? 7

4 Managing Your Folio

Managing your folio 8

5 Writing Prose Fiction

Short story structure 10
Beginning to plan: outlines, plots and themes 12
The who: creating characters 14
The where and when: creating the setting 16
The what: constructing narrative 18
The how: creating narrative viewpoint 19
Getting started: the introduction 20
The body paragraphs 23
The ending 23
Short story? Or an episode from a novel? 24
How convincing is my fiction? 25

6 Writing Poetry

The poetry option	26
Working in sonnet form	28
The sonnet in Scotland	30
Free verse	32

7 Scriptwriting

The scriptwriting option	36
Page layout	42
Sketch	43
Monologue	44

8 Discursive Writing

The discursive family	46
Argumentative/persuasive: what tools do they use?	47
Checking out persuasive writing	47
Planning, researching and plagiarism	50
Structuring and sequencing	53
Introductions	55
The discursive body paragraph	57
Argumentative/persuasive: the conclusion	60
How well am I arguing my case?	61
The final checklist	63

9 Report Writing

How do reports fit into the discursive family?	64
How does a report differ from an essay?	65
Making a start	66
Presenting your report	69
How does all this look in practice?	70
Alternative approaches to report writing	71

10 Personal Reflective Essay

Personal reflective essay	72
Putting it all together	73
So what shall I write about?	75
Planning effectively	76
Getting started	78

11 Editing Your Text

Editing your text	81

12 Vocabulary

Increase your word power	84
Complete the sentence (1)	84
Working with definitions (1)	85
Word substitution (1)	86
Making a critical collocation (1)	87
Complete the sentence (2)	88
Working with definitions (2)	89
Word substitution (2)	90
Making a critical collocation (2)	91

Answers

	92

Introduction

Welcome

By this stage in your academic career, you will be no stranger to writing essays. Whatever SQA route you took to arrive here, your teachers will have placed considerable emphasis throughout on sound essay writing skills. We have structured this guide to the Higher and Intermediate 2 writing folio expressly to take those hard-won skills to the next stage of development so that you achieve the best final grade possible.

With the writing folio you will be demonstrating to external assessors what you can achieve through the reflective and drafting process. The introduction of the folio means that your final grade no longer depends exclusively on your performance in close reading and critical essays on the day of the exam itself. This will be good news for many.

While the help offered here is aimed at your success in the English writing folio, remember that you can transfer many of the skills developed here to English exams, NABs and other subject areas where essay writing skills are vital.

The ability to write convincingly, in whatever genre, is the cornerstone of all academic success. Writing skills need to be mastered if your views are to be taken seriously, both at school and beyond.

This guide will not just **tell** you *what* is required but **show** you *how* to go about doing it, so you can improve your performance and get the results you want.

What the writing folio involves

You will be required to submit a folio of two writing pieces, one being broadly creative, the other broadly discursive.

Creative outcomes

The creative outcomes are sub-divided into four genres:

- a personal reflective essay
- a piece of prose fiction, such as a short story or episode from a novel
- a poem or set of thematically linked poems
- a dramatic script, such as a scene, a monologue or sketch

Discursive outcomes

The discursive outcomes are sub-divided into three genres:

- a persuasive essay
- an argumentative essay
- a report

There are word limits which must be respected. Failure to do so will mean your work will be penalised.

	Minimum	Maximum
Higher	650 words	1300 words
Intermediate 2	500 words	1000 words

Poems, however, are not subject to the minimum length requirement.

How the folio is assessed

Like your critical essays in the examination itself, the folio pieces will each be marked out of 25. When these marks are turned into part of your total percentage, you will find that the writing folio counts for 20% of your final grade, with close reading contributing 40% and critical essays 40%.

How the writing folio affects your language study unit

Your language study unit has traditionally consisted of a close reading NAB and a writing piece. You will continue to produce a writing piece for this unit. You may, however, use your folio piece twice: first, as the writing outcome for the LSU which you submit for the internal pass or fail assessment; later, you may submit this again as a folio piece for external assessment. If you enjoy writing, you may, of course, write three different pieces: one for internal assessment, the other two for external assessment.

Be careful, however, if you are thinking of using an essay twice. The submission date for the writing folio is April. By April, you will probably feel that the essay skills you have developed over the year will bring you a much better written outcome than one produced earlier in the academic year.

How your performance is assessed

Your essays will be measured against the performance criteria below. These differ from Intermediate 2 to Higher. Make sure you have them in mind at all stages of the drafting and re-drafting process.

INTERMEDIATE 2	HIGHER
Content: This should be relevant and appropriate for its purpose and audience. It should reveal some depth and complexity of thought and some sustained development.	**Content:** This should be relevant and appropriate for its purpose and audience. It should reveal depth and complexity of thought and sustained development.
Structure: This should take account of purpose, audience and genre. The content should be sequenced and organised in ways which are mainly effective.	**Structure:** The structure should be effective and appropriate for purpose, audience and genre. The content should be sequenced and organised in ways which assist impact.
Expression: Here, competent use of techniques relevant to the genre and appropriate choice of words and sentence structures should establish a style and tone which communicate a point of view/stance consistent with purpose and audience.	**Expression:** Here, capable use of techniques relevant to the genre and effective choice of words and sentence structures should sustain a style and tone which clearly communicate a point of view/stance consistent with purpose and audience.
Technical accuracy: Here, a few errors may be present, but these will not be significant in any way. You may use some complex vocabulary and sentence structures. Where appropriate, sentences will show accurate handling of clauses. Linking sentences will be clear. Paragraphing will reflect a developing line of thought.	**Technical accuracy:** Here, few errors will be present. Paragraphs, sentences and punctuation are accurate and organised so that writing can be clearly and readily understood. Spelling errors (particularly of high frequency words) should be infrequent.

Remember, too, that a piece of writing which does not satisfy the requirements for 'consistent' technical accuracy cannot pass. If, however, technical accuracy is deemed 'consistent', there will be no penalties or deductions for any errors.

Throughout this guide you will find that we are here to make sure you are fully supported in meeting these demanding criteria. So let's get started!

What's the difference between a folio piece and an exam room essay?

In a word: time. In the exam, you are writing a critical essay under pressure. Your eye is constantly on the clock. The folio piece, whether discursive or creative, will be produced according to a schedule agreed between you and your teacher over a number of weeks. This timescale for the folio essay allows you the opportunity to demonstrate your abilities to the full, free of exam room pressure. You need to make the most of this. Let's look at how essay writing in the two areas may differ before considering how to make the most of the opportunities offered by the drafting and re-drafting process.

WHAT'S EXPECTED OF A FOLIO ESSAY?	WHAT'S EXPECTED OF AN EXAM ROOM ESSAY?
1. Since the time frame here is fairly generous, the examiner will expect an extended, well-structured piece, with the topic fully explored. Discursive pieces should show evidence of adequate research. Reflective/creative essays should demonstrate a full awareness of writing techniques.	1. Given the limited time available here, 'fully explored' should perhaps read 'as fully as possible'.
2. A clear line of development should be apparent, with the steps in your discussion/argument/story being signalled from paragraph to paragraph. Check this with each draft.	2. You should aim for a similarly apparent line of development, although, given the shortage of time, it will be understood if your structure is not quite as polished as that in a folio piece.
3. It should include an introduction that captures the examiner's interest. In a discursive essay it should explain any background necessary to understanding the topic. The conclusion should summarise the main ideas touched on. In reflective/creative pieces the introduction and ending, although quite different from those of a discursive piece, should provide equally interesting and satisfying reading experiences.	3. The introduction should make clear your approach to answering the question and give the examiner sufficient detail of the upcoming discussion, including a reference to the wording of the question. Time may restrict as full a conclusion as you might wish for, but you should aim to round off your essay with some return, however brief, to the wording of the question.
4. Your approach should enhance your ideas in terms of suitable vocabulary, clear expression, grammar, spelling, typing. Tone and style should be appropriate. Bibliographic referencing (where required) should be accurate and consistent.	4. Tone, style and vocabulary should show familiarity with the critical essay genre.

Managing your folio

As you start to prepare your folio you will be increasingly aware that the date for your Intermediate 2 or Higher English exam is creeping ever closer. So, too, are exams in other subjects. This is a moment when there will be multiple pressures on your time. It is all the more essential, therefore, that you organise your folio preparation time sensibly.

Agreeing a timetable

Your starting point needs to be a timetable (agreed with your teacher) for the various stages through which your work has to pass before final submission. This is necessary to ensure your teacher is regularly in touch with your work to establish its authenticity. It is also essential that its timings should be respected if you are to meet the submission deadline comfortably. A folio worth 20% of your final grade cannot be rushed!

Candidate's log

The folio is an exercise which, in its encouragement of independent study, is a useful preparation for the world of college and university. A log such as the following one is a valuable tool in helping you plan and stick to a schedule which will ensure your workload does not get out-of-hand.

Draft proposals Scheduled date:	Teacher's comments:
Outline plan Scheduled date:	Teacher's comments:
First draft Scheduled date:	Teacher's comments:
Second draft Scheduled date:	Teacher's comments:

Getting started

Once your timetable is agreed it's time to settle down to the question of genres to be considered. No easy task! This is the moment when this *Success Guide* comes into its own.

Go through it, checking out the kinds of writing which attract you and in which you may already have shown some ability. Do you feel most comfortable reflecting on some aspect of your personal experience? Or are you attracted to creating a short story? Maybe you enjoy engaging with ideas in an argumentative or persuasive essay?

List potential genres and consider fully the pros and cons of each one. Spend considerable time on this stage before even thinking of a specific title or topic, before planning or drafting a single word. Time well spent here will save you a lot of time later on.

Remember, however, that the folio at this level will demand a degree of writing skills more polished than those you may have demonstrated earlier in your career. So make sure you make the most of the writing tips offered for each genre. There's a wealth of ideas here waiting to be explored.

Consulting regularly

As independence of study is being encouraged, there is a limit to the help your teacher is allowed to offer. So, suggestions will usually be general rather than detailed. If, for example, you are told that the structure of your argumentative essay is weak, go back to see what the *Success Guide* has to say about this. Or, if your teacher thinks the setting of your short story is unconvincing, check out what practical advice the guide has to give about enriching it. It's all here. Make the most of it, whatever genre you select.

Editing the final draft

Before you hand in either of your two drafts, go to the 'Editing Your Text' section of this guide, on page 81. It is a valuable mine of practical help about how to avoid making the kind of mistake that could bring you down in the eyes of the examiner.

Glitches creep in, particularly in a drafted text which has been changed at various stages. Mistakes happen, even in the work of the best writers.

Check your work over until you have a document which you feel confident does full justice to your abilities and which you can hand in with, yes, an element of real pride. Go for it!

Writing prose fiction

Short story structure

For your folio you have the choice of a short story or an episode from a novel. We will look first at the short story. Structure apart, however, much of what can be said about many of its elements can be said of all good prose fiction. For successful fiction requires sound characterisation, convincing setting and a narrative viewpoint that fits the task in hand, whether it be in a short story or in an episode from a novel.

Some writing guides will tell you that a good working structure is:

Top Tip

Don't attempt *Star Wars* in a short story. Out, too, are family sagas stretching over generations. Keep the number of characters limited and the time scale modest: weeks, days, even hours.

a settled situation involving two or three figures;
a complication brought about by a new element, perhaps the appearance of a new character or the arrival of a letter;
a rising tension brought about by the changed situation;
a crisis which results in **a turning point** in the fortunes of the characters; and
a change in situation, relationship, understanding or viewpoint.

While such a structure is true of many short stories, remember that there are many others which respect only some of these elements. Should you feel, however, that this kind of structure is a helpful one for you, do not hesitate to use it. But since every word is important in a short story, make sure you do not introduce actions or incidents that have no bearing on the overall outcome of the story. (An exception might be when an action or incident helps you understand a character better.)

Top Tip

All actions in a short story must either have a bearing on the plot or on the illustration of character.

What is important about whatever structure you choose is that readers should finish the story feeling you have offered them a rich reading experience. **Believable characters** should be engaged in a series of **credible situations** which **develop convincingly** before being **concluded satisfyingly**. In many short stories the satisfying conclusion often involves change of some kind: in the fortunes or happiness of the character(s), in their perceptions of themselves and their world or in how they are perceived by other people, including the reader. If there is no change of any kind, you risk the reader quitting the story saying, 'So what?'

Quick Task

Here are a few crises that could be the turning points in a short story. With a partner or in a group, discuss what might have led up to each situation, who the principal characters might be, why the crisis occurred and what might be the resulting outcome. Sketch out an outline for what you think the story might be and present it to the class for comment.

1. *The classroom door swung open, revealing Mrs Mitchell, one of the depute headteachers. Hurriedly, she crossed to the desk to whisper something urgently to Biggsy. He turned pure white, looking at her in disbelief before virtually racing out of the room. 'Mr Biggs may not be returning this period or even ...' Frowning, Mrs Mitchell broke off. 'A cover teacher will be here shortly. This is nothing that need concern you,' she added, somewhat unconvincingly.*

2. *'It's your Tom,' said her sister Josephine, putting down the phone gently. 'There's been a terrible accident. One of the shafts has collapsed. They think he was in that part of the mine when it happened. You will have to be brave.'*

3. *The court official looked at the woman. 'I see you haven't paid the fine. You will have to go to court now or the police will be here for you. And what will happen to your children if you go to jail?' The woman turned pale. Clearly, she was at her wit's end. 'But I can't. I just can't,' she wailed, like an animal in pain.*

4. *'You have stayed with them long enough,' Gina cried. 'You are virtually their prisoner. Yes, they are kind to you, but your future is elsewhere now. You needed them once, but that time is long past. Come away with me. I have tickets for London. That's where your future lies.' Bruno hesitated, then slowly, reluctantly, reached for his battered case. She was right.*

Top Tip

The best way to write good short stories is to read as many of them as you can. As you read, pay particular attention to how the structure and plot work.

For your interest, 2 is very loosely based on a short story by Kate Chopin called 'The Story of an Hour', 3 is similarly sketched around 'The Tax Gatherer' by Neil M. Gunn and 4 owes its origin to 'Ladies in Lavender' by William J. Locke. Try to find the stories in question. (The Kate Chopin story is available online; 'Ladies in Lavender' was turned into a successful film starring Maggie Smith and Judi Dench.)

Were your suggestions anywhere near the facts of the original? It would be interesting if they were, but your ideas are equally valid if they hang together persuasively.

Beginning to plan: outlines, plots and themes

Before you start your own short story you would be well advised to work on an outline, rather in the way you did in that last quick task but in a bit more detail. You need to be sure of what you want to include in your story before you embark on the writing. In other words, work out what is to happen in your story, who is involved, when and where it takes place. You may not be sure yet of the detail but an outline helps shape your thinking about people, places and events. Draw up a table similar to the one that follows and use it to outline roughly your first thoughts.

WHO?	Two friends? Mother and son? Employer and employee? Homeless person and banker? Rivals in love? A happy/unhappy couple? Passengers on a train? Teacher and pupil? Roughly outline personality and appearance for now. Details can come later.
WHEN?	Is it set in the present day, the past or the future? Will the time of day, the season or the weather be important for adding to the atmosphere? Will these factors *change* in the course of the story?
WHERE?	Like your cast list, this cannot be allowed to get out of hand in a short story. Decide on a setting you can describe really well. Don't set it in the Palace of Versailles or the slums of New York unless you know these places really well. Try surroundings you are familiar with – and don't move around too much. A settled, well-described atmosphere will be an important ingredient in your story's success. Think of films you have enjoyed because the director knew the setting intimately.
WHAT?	You need to be sure in your own mind of the sequence of events. But are you going to *tell* the story in this sequence? Or are you going to use flash-forward/flash-back techniques? In other words, you need to work out in rough the manner in which the plot is to advance.
HOW?	How is this story to be told? Is the narrator to be 'I'? Or are you going to use the third-person narrative, i.e. 'he' or 'she'?

There is one very important aspect of a successful story at which we have still to look: its *theme*. We could describe this as the 'why?' of the story.

WHY?	Plot is *what* happens in your story. Theme tells us why you wrote it in the first place. Your theme is what you have to say about an idea which you wish to share with your readers. The theme is what the story is *about*.
	For example, the short story 'Mossy' by Audrey Evans has as its plot the story of the last hours of a teacher before she retires, but it is *about* how little we know of people behind their public face.
	You need to consider the idea of theme from the start of your story. With theme, you can be making a point about all sorts of things: love, friendship, ambition, prejudice, jealousy, courage, revenge, broken society, the basic decency of human nature or whatever it is that sparked your story.
	Theme works best if you can underline it in more than one way. Perhaps it can be underpinned by the setting. Perhaps it touches the lives of more than one person in the story. This is an idea we will return to later.

Top Tip

Plot is what happens in the story; theme is what the story is about. For your short story to be successful, you need to consider both of these fully before starting your first draft.

Quick Task

What comes most naturally to you? In creating a story outline, do you tend to think of the theme *first* and *then* work out plot details to illustrate this theme? Or does it happen the other way round? Discuss the relative merits of each approach with a partner or in a group.

The who: creating characters

If we expect readers to be interested in the fate of our characters, we need to make them more than simply a name. We need to make them as believable as we can.

Here is how Scottish writer Denise Mina describes one of her characters:

> Carol Brady didn't have an attractive face. She was very wrinkled but didn't look like she'd got that way having fun. Her eyelids were drooping, resting on her stubby eye-lashes and pushing them down. Behind the little curtains of skin her eyes were raw with the shocked despair of a recent death in the family. Her brown hair was thinning and meshed together with hair-spray like a lacy crash helmet.
>
> (*Garnethill.* Denise Mina. Bantam Books 1998)

As in personal reflective writing, detail is of prime importance in creating characters. Carol Brady may not be a very pleasant human being, but we feel as if she is right in front of us. We can *see* her, thanks to Mina's skill in handling detail. Yet, this 'head shot' is all we get to learn of her appearance: no mention of physical build or clothes. Nevertheless, it establishes her character well. Look what we learn about Brady in 70 words. This kind of economy is important in short story writing.

'very wrinkled but didn't look like she'd got that way having fun'	Calendar years unspecified but in unhappy middle-age at least. Grim outlook on life hinted at but not stated.
'eyelids were drooping, resting on her stubby eyelashes and pushing them down. Behind the little curtains of skin ...'	Note the original word choice of 'little curtains of skin'. 'Curtains' may carry connotations of concealment. 'Drooping' eyelids add to the notion that Brady is not perhaps exactly direct in her gaze – or even in life?
'... her eyes were raw with shocked despair of a recent death ...'	Shorthand explanation of recent events in her life. Capable of strong feeling.
'... hair was thinning and meshed together ... like a lacy crash helmet.'	Despite advancing age, or perhaps because of it, a lingering vanity, captured with a highly original simile.

Before you can begin to construct such a character description you need to get to know your character in detail. Devise your own table to accommodate as many characters as you plan to engage in the story. Gather as much information as you can at this stage. You may not use it all in the story, but the character becomes more real in your own mind and thus easier to write about and convey to your readers. Here are just some areas you may wish to explore. Perhaps you can add some of your own.

Top Tip

Remember that conflict and contrast between characters drives forward stories. Have you allowed for that in your cast of characters?

	CHARACTER ONE	CHARACTER TWO
Name		
Age		
Appearance (4/5 adjectives)		
Personality (4/5 adjectives)		
Interests/hobbies		

Musical tastes		
Home life/family		
Friends		
Occupation		
Success in life		

Show as well as tell

Be very alert to how you present character information in your story. For instance, personality can sometimes come across more powerfully when you are *shown* it in action rather than just *told* about it. You can sometimes illustrate a personality trait by the character's behaviour in a situation instead of by description alone.

Kindness, for example, can be powerfully conveyed by a character picking up a walking stick dropped by a pensioner; aggression can be shown by the forceful stamping out of a cigarette.

It is a sound idea to mix both approaches to create well-rounded characters.

 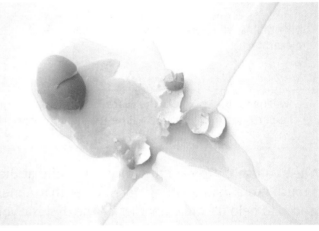

Quick Task

With a partner, invent brief actions in a story which might illustrate the following characteristics. Once you have decided what the actions might be, write the sentence(s) which would convey this in a short story. Do not mention any of the words in the table. Did your partner guess the characteristic correctly from your text?

cruelty	anxiety
generosity	impatience
courage	affection

Top Tip

Basing your characters loosely on people you know may help you bring them to life: mannerisms, ways of talking and dress sense may all prove useful.

The where and when: creating the setting

Just as successful character creation is grounded in detail, so too is setting. Here is part of the setting of a short story called 'Hieroglyphics' by another Scottish writer, Anne Donovan.

> A big rid brick building bloackin oot the sky. Spiky railins wi green paint peelin aff them. Hard grey tarmac space wi weans loupin aw ower the place, playin chasies in the yerd, joukin aboot roond the teachers' motors; the big yins sophisticated, hingin aboot the corner, huvin a fly puff afore the bell goes. And us, wee furst years, aw shiny an poalished-lookin in wur new uniforms (soon tae be discardit), staunin in front ae the main door, waitin tae be tellt where we're gaun.
>
> (*Hieroglyphics and other stories*. Anne Donovan. Canongate 2001)

The detail catches not only the thoughts of this new first-year pupil, it hints at the writer's attitude to this educational world as seen through the eyes of young Mary.

'big rid brick building bloakin oot the sky.'	This school building is getting in the way of the light. What might this hint about the writer's view of education?
'Spiky railins wi green paint peelin aff them. Hard grey tarmac ...'	The sharpness of the railings and the hardness of the tarmac create a hostile environment for small children. The peeling paint and greyness add their own grimness.
'.... weans loupin aw ower the place, playin chasies in the yerd, joukin aboot roond the teachers' motors ...'	Despite the bleak environment, there is a natural resilience and energy in the children which is uncrushed by it.

When you go on to read the story you find that the setting here is much more than a setting, for you see that Anne Donovan has used it to help illustrate her *theme*. The dyslexic young Mary, you learn, has the natural inventiveness and resilience to triumph over an education system which has failed her badly. The playground setting underpins the writer's theme of the deadening power of education and children's capacity to overcome it. When you write your own story, think about how setting can be useful in illustrating *your* theme.

Now let's go back to that table we mentioned on page 13. You are in a position to construct a detailed table which considers your setting in depth, a setting which not only creates atmosphere but may also underline your theme.

	POINTS TO CONSIDER	YOUR DETAILS
Place	Type of building/street/town as backdrop? Name of street or town? Leafy and prosperous? Grim and broken down? Countryside? High moorlands? Forest? Seaside? Britain or abroad?	
Time	Today? The future? Distant past? Recent past? Set against the background of an historical event? Be careful if you are going to go into the past: you will need to do some research. What is the time frame of your story from start to finish? A day? A week? A holiday?	
Season	How is this to be established? Shown or told? Will winter be used for a bleak tale or a heart-warming one set around Christmas? Will high summer mark the high spot in a relationship and winter its low point or end? How could spring or autumn be used?	
Weather	Will it have a bearing on the mood of the character/scene? Heavy rain? Frost? Gales? Hot and clammy? Thundery? Bitterly cold? Will it change as the fortunes of the character(s) change(s)? Will it underline their mood sympathetically or be in complete contrast to it, seemingly indifferent?	

Are there other aspects of the setting that may be important for *your* story which are not mentioned here? Add them to your table now.

Top Tip

Consider settings you know really well if you are finding it difficult to conjure up imaginary places. The reader will find your story more convincing if you use a real-life setting.

Quick Task

Think about settings which might be suitable for the following short stories. List at least six details of time and place you might wish to include.

A story about a 58 year old woman who is told she has a possibly life-threatening illness.
A story about a simmering row between a young couple, which finally erupts.
A story about a child who is frightened of going to sleep in the dark.

The what: constructing narrative

In an earlier part of this section on prose fiction we looked at the difference between plot and theme.

Theme, as we said, is what the story is *about*. Suppose your theme is a criticism of the throwaway society in which we seem to live. How could we develop such a theme?

Theme comes across strongest when it is illustrated on several levels. For example, you might have a central character who loses his job, after many years with the same company, because the company decides it is easier/cheaper to re-train a younger person. You could also introduce his son/daughter who is considering divorce after only a short period of marriage, an example of a different kind of relationship being disposed of when it becomes inconvenient. Underpinning this theme, you might have the story begin with this character walking to work past a discarded sofa or television awaiting the rubbish collection, long before he learns of his fate. In ways like this the theme can be illuminated for readers. They see it touching the lives of more than one person and being symbolised in the setting itself.

Some people may wish to work by considering a theme in this way. Others may prefer to start with a situation involving characters and wait to see what theme emerges from their interaction.

Whatever method you choose, now is the time to brainstorm credible outlines for your story.

Once you have decided on a story outline, your next decision is to decide how the story is to advance.

- Are you going to start at the beginning and work your way through events chronologically?

- Are you going to begin with a flash-forward before retreating to a time in the past when the story began? Such an approach offers you an exciting opening; indeed, it might be the crisis or turning point of the story itself.

- Are you going to begin at the end, describing outcomes and then flash back to a more chronological narrative?

The best way to decide may be to experiment with various methods to see which one you are most comfortable with and which seems to work well with your story.

Quick Task

You have an idea for a story involving two teenage girls/boys, close friends since primary school, who fall out rather badly. Brainstorm with a partner as many ideas as you can for what the theme might be. Which idea would make the most convincing theme for *you*, were you to write this story?

Could you think of an outline for such a story? It is good to practise this kind of exercise before you start on your short story in earnest.

The how: creating narrative viewpoint

So how is your story to be told? Is the story to be told by a narrator, an 'I' figure? Or is the reader to be an onlooker, watching the action as it unfolds? Conventionally, there are usually two choices: first-person narrative or third-person narrative, although third person can be sub-divided into two branches as shown below. What are the relative benefits and limitations of each approach?

	BENEFITS	LIMITATIONS
First-person narrative Here the narrator is a participant in the story and tells it from his/her point of view. *I looked around me. Would the train ever arrive? And where was she? She had said she would be here by four.*	You are invited into the narrator's innermost thoughts and feelings. You can come really close to the narrator as you share his/her experience at first hand by seeing everything through his/her eyes.	You are shut out of what may be going on in the head of other characters in the story. Nor do you see what they are up to when you are not present in the scene.
Third-person narrative (subjective version) Here the story unfolds as seen from the viewpoint of a certain character in the story. *Lawrence looked around him, wondering if the train would ever arrive. He was feeling restive now. Where was she? She had said she would be there by four.*	As with the 'I' approach, you are close to the private thoughts and feelings of one of the story's characters. The reader tends to sympathise with the person through whose eyes he/she views events.	This character has to be present at all happenings in the story so they can be reported. This may hinder a full examination of events in a short story where word limits apply.
Third-person narrative (objective version) *Lawrence looked around him. The platform clock struck four. He moved slowly over to a bench and sat down. He tapped his foot on the ground restlessly, looking up regularly at the platform clock.*	The story unfolds with a camera-like objectivity. Everything about a scene is recorded. We are present in the lives and actions of all the characters, but merely as onlookers.	We are not invited into the character's mental experiences. We must assess these from external behavioural signs.

Top Tip

Before you decide on a narrative viewpoint, try out a short section of your story using *all* the narrative methods described here. Which one worked best for you and your story?

Getting started: the introduction

Now that you have in place the framework of your story, your next task is to launch the story in a way that will hook your readers. So how is this to be done? Here are some ideas from the work of successful short story writers. They have, for convenience, been divided up into some favourite approaches.

The voice

With this approach a personality is instantly captured in the 'voice' which is conjured up. Note that successfully capturing a voice may involve re-ordering the words to follow speech patterns rather than written patterns.

> I tell you what it is. I sit here night after night and he sits there night after night. In that chair opposite me. The two of us. I'm eighty years old and he's eighty four. And that's what we do, we sit and think.

('Napoleon and I' in *Selected Stories*. Ian Crichton Smith. Carcanet Press 1990)

> I love my kids. My husband too, though sometimes he asks me whether I do; asks the question, Do you still love me? He asks me it while I am in the middle of rinsing spinach or loading washing into the machine, or chasing a trail of toys around the kitchen floor.

('All The Little Loved Ones' in *Red Tides*. Dilys Rose. Random House UK/Martin Secker and Warburg)

> I used to be a road digger, which is to say I dug up roads for a living. These days I'm a Repair Effecter for the council's Highways Department. I still dig up the roads – sorry, highways – only now it sounds better, doesn't it?

('A Deep Hole' in *Beggars Banquet*. Ian Rankin. Orion 2002)

- Readers are hooked by this approach since you are reaching out from your story in your 'I' voice and talking to them directly. They cannot help but be engaged.
- Be careful to continue your story in the guise of your adopted persona. This will need adjusting perhaps when you complete your first draft. Is your tone of voice and, through it, your personality consistent throughout? Or if it changes, is that change intentional?

The tease

Here your aim is to intrigue the reader by constructing an opening that puzzles in some way. 'What is going on here?', is the reader's first response. He/she wants to know what is to follow.

> Ah mind they were birlin and dancin roond like big black spiders. Ah couldnae keep a haunle on them fur every time ah thoat ah'd captured them, tied them thegither in some kindy order, they jist kept on escapin.

('Hieroglyphics' in *Hieroglyphics and other stories*. Anne Donovan. Canongate 2001)

> My father sits on the bed in the bedroom at the back of the house, one hand just brushing on the raised ridges of the candlewick cover over the continental quilt, the other holding a pair of women's pants coloured a very light pink.

('A story of folding and unfolding' in *Free Love and other stories*. Ali Smith. Virago 1995)

> They'd be watching and waiting for her back at the house. Zoe would be twisting her hair by the attic window, listening to the rain and trying to work out what time she must have left. Her mother would have The Archers on without listening to it ... She could picture her father, too, chopping peppers into even slices, marinating the beef ... And Tomas. He'd be reassuring them that she was just out for a walk ... And he'd have hidden the baby clothes at the back of the airing cupboard, lifted the cot into the attic.

('The Black Devon' in *In the Event of Fire*. Corinne Fowler. ASLS 2009)

- Here you commit readers to your story by tantalising them in some way. The situation only gradually becomes clear. Explanation may, although not necessarily, arrive by a flash-back of some kind; it may also occur through additional information becoming available as the narrative progresses.
- You need to be sure that your story stands up to the boldness of the opening and what follows is not an anti-climax.

The scene

By simply describing the opening location of your story, you are following in the steps of many film-makers who open with a shot which captures time and place. Gradually, characters are brought into the scene.

> The first ferry for a week was fast to the quay, the thick rope springs holding it to, looped fore and aft over iron cleats the height of children. The weather had been so hard and high that there was seaweed all over the island, brought in by the wind, and the east wall of each house was drifted up to the roof.

('The Only Only' in *New Writing 3*. Candia McWilliams. Gillon Aitken Associates/Minerva 1994)

> The house stood on the north side of the courtyard. It was pleasantly neat and the door was closed, locked, and painted green. The shutters were folded quickly over the windows. A yellow mat of plaited grass hung on the parapet of a well. Beside the well a bucket and a coil of chain shone with a clean pewter colour.

('A House in Sicily' in *The Penguin Book of Scottish Short Stories*. Neil McCallum. 1970)

> That was a fine Saturday afternoon. The town was full of tourists in light-coloured clothes, white and pink and lilac, like baby clothes. There were a lot of pale legs around, and varicose veins and bellies; but there were some goodlookers too, most of them young.

('Between Man and Woman Keys' in *Three Kinds of Kissing*. Rosalind Brackenbury. HarperCollins 1993)

- This is perhaps the most straightforward of introductions. If you feel a 'clever' introduction is too difficult, this method may be helpful. From this well-grounded setting your story can gradually grow.
- For its success, this approach depends on convincing scene-painting detail. Make sure, as in personal reflective writing, your detail is strong enough for the reader to visualise your scene vividly.

The character

Some writers focus first on a character as a means of leading the reader into the action.

> Miss Caldwell was the smarter of the pair. At one time customers would tell her she looked like Rosalind Russell. Even in retirement she had kept her figure (with difficulty) and always wore a turban (in the French style) and good accessories and shoes.

('Paris' in The *Devil and the Giro*. Ronald Frame. Canongate 1989)

> Thea Docherty left Glasgow for Barlochan in September of 1937. She rented a house on the outskirts of the village. With two children and no husband in evidence, she was a subject of talk from the day she arrived.

('South America' in *Secret Villages*. Douglas Dunn. Faber and Faber 1985)

> The village street is deserted. From the far end, where the bus stops, a girl walks up the pavement, weighed down with bags. On this autumn day she wears a thin floral dress, hiking boots and a nose ring. A gust of cold stirs the tangles of her bleached hair and makes goosebumps rise on her skin.

('Her Mother's Songs' in *The Dynamics of Balsa*. Merryn Glover. ASLS 2007)

- Appearance and standing in the community are what the authors here chose to lead with in their presentation of their main characters. These might be useful starting points for you, too.
- Again, detail is necessary for an opening that catches the reader's attention and imagination.

The event

Here the story starts without any preliminary description, but simply begins in the middle of an event happening. The action is intended to capture the reader's attention and only later are other details of character and place filled in.

> Two men in T-shirts got out of the van and one opened its back door and climbed in. They unloaded the bench, shifting the weight to and from each other, first to get it out of the van and then as a kind of game, calling to each other when one caught the other out.

('College' in *Free Love and other stories*. Ali Smith. Virago 1995)

Top Tip

Find an anthology of short stories in your library. Browse through it, noting how published authors solve some of the problems you may be mulling over. Check introductory paragraphs in particular.

> The body when he found it wasn't unlike the ones he'd seen pictures of sticking out of the ice when the glaciers retreated. He wouldn't have found it at all but for a break in the clouds that had draped themselves about the hills since morning, casting sudden shafts of sunlight along the Bad Dearg perimeter.

('Fallers' in *The Dynamics of Balsa*. Andy Manders. ASLS 2007)

> Just when he was maybe beginning to fall asleep at last, George Lockhart, an insomniac, thought he heard something bumping softly against his door. He opened his eyes to the darkness and listened. There it was again, against the door of his flat, soft but insistent.

('A Good Night's Sleep' in *Under Cover*. Brian McCabe. Mainstream Publishing 1993)

- The event itself can be dramatic, like the finding of a body, or it can be fairly ordinary, like moving a bench.
- The action involved plunges the reader immediately into an ongoing situation which will require explanation in upcoming paragraphs.

As this very brief round-up of introductory approaches will have suggested to you, there are as many approaches to introductions as there are stories.

The body paragraphs

As you follow your plan of the story, keep checking on your word count. Ensure that you are not devoting too much attention to one section of the story in a way that will mean other sections may end up sounding hasty and unconvincing.

Is your plan working? As you write, it may appear that your characters are developing a life of their own. Perhaps you have had a better idea of how their fates may be resolved. If this is the case, follow your instincts. But re-draft the plan in the light of these developments. You still need an overall structure that keeps you on track for the word count.

Try to keep the story moving so that each paragraph moves the narrative on in some way. Detail is vitally important, but it cannot be allowed to interrupt the flow of what you have to say.

In your present course, when examining texts and practising exercises in textual analysis, you are spending considerable time discussing published writers' use of language. Are you putting what you are learning about the persuasive power of metaphors, similes, personification, alliteration, etc. to good use in your own writing? Be careful not to indulge in these simply for their own sake but, well placed, they can lift the quality of your prose immeasurably.

The ending

Here is where the interaction of your characters is finally resolved. This resolution should flow naturally from the events you've described. Don't impose an ending which may seem forced. Don't leave too many loose ends, but don't make your ending sound contrived and unconvincing either.

As we mentioned earlier, change should be in the air here. It may be that roles have been reversed in some way: the earlier underdog is now on top; the fortunes of the lucky/unlucky have changed; the miserable have found happiness of some kind, or vice-versa. It may simply be that characters now view themselves differently from their initial self-assessment; it may be that others in the story view them differently; it may be that we, the readers, view the central character(s) in some new light.

Stylistically, this is where you can make a good impression. Can you make a link here with some feature of the opening?

- A remark that was made at the start is made again, but in a changed context it may have taken on a subtly different meaning.
- A detail that was mentioned earlier is referred to again but altered: a door that opened now closes; a once-dripping tap no longer drips (or perhaps it continues to do so); music that was heard earlier re-appears; a painting that was being embarked upon at the story's start is now finished.
- The opening paragraph may be repeated, but with a significant change at one point.

The list is endless according to the circumstances of your tale. Such stylistic touches suggest the story has come satisfyingly – and *elegantly* – full circle.

Short story? Or an episode from a novel?

For your work of fiction, the folio gives you the choice between a short story and an episode from a novel.

While there is nothing to stop you writing a chapter from the middle or the end of the novel, realistically, many people may well decide on the opening section of a novel since it requires no explanation other than itself to make sense to the reader. Starting in the middle of events will pose wordy problems of explanation for you and difficulties of comprehension for your readers as they attempt to piece together what has gone before.

So how will your approach differ in tackling a short story and the opening chapter of a novel?

You will no doubt be relieved to hear that much of what has been said about a short story also applies to all good prose writing, including the opening chapter of a novel.

This said, there will be differences, quite significant ones, so let's take a look at what is shared between the two genres and ways in which they differ.

	SHORT STORY	OPENING CHAPTER OF NOVEL
Plot/structure	CLOSED STRUCTURE By the time readers come to the end of your narrative, they will have been offered a narrative complete in itself with a beginning, a middle and an end.	OPEN STRUCTURE By the time readers come to the end of your narrative, plot lines will have been set in motion but not in any way resolved. Markers, however, will have been left as to possible story lines. If, say, a relationship is unsatisfactory: will the partners remain together or seek happiness elsewhere? Are there clues to later choices? If a business is failing: will it be saved or will it go bankrupt? Hints either way can be planted.
Characters	Here, characters have to establish their personalities fully in the course of the story. Any changes envisaged in them have to be achieved in the course of the narrative.	Here, while the major outlines of the characters' personalities need to have been established, there should be room for development in following chapters. Hints may be left as to future behaviour. For example, a decent character may have a hasty temper which could later lead to trouble. Friendship between characters may be seen to be somewhat superficial which may suggest later upsets.
Setting	Here, a short story and the opening chapter of a novel have similar needs. Both require the reader to believe entirely in the credibility of the setting, so time and place must be well-grounded.	Freed from the necessity of completing your narrative in the chapter of the novel, you may have scope for place/weather/seasons to be more fully explored.
Narrative voice	Here also, short stories and novel chapters have much in common. Decide which narrative voice is most convincing for your situation.	Given that the novel chapter does not require full resolution, you have more space to experiment with different narrative voices. Perhaps we can hear from different narrative voices in the course of the chapter?

How convincing is my fiction?

Don't be in too much of a hurry to hand in your drafts. Go over each one in detail, asking yourself what criticisms could be levelled at it. Can you improve it before your teacher sees it?

Are the events in my outline appropriate for a piece with my word limit?
Is my outline credible/interesting? Lacking in incidents? Perhaps with too many incidents?
Is my theme clear?
Are my characters grounded in sufficient detail to make them believable?
Is there sufficient contrast between my characters to make their relationship dynamic?
Is my setting persuasive? Do I need to add more detail or do I have too much for this length of story?
Are there moments when the writing stops moving forward? If there are, what can be done about this?
Does the narrative viewpoint selected seem the correct one for the task in hand?
Is the ending of my short story well-handled? Will readers feel satisfied by the resolution?
Have I managed to insert into the closing paragraphs of the short story some stylistic device that signals stylish completion to the reader?
Elsewhere, have I introduced sufficient elements of style (metaphors, similes, personification, etc.) to enhance my storyline?

Writing Poetry

The poetry option

> Good poems are written because they have to be, not because their authors want them to be.
>
> James Reeves

This is a daunting thought for anyone contemplating writing a poem or a set of thematically linked poems for the folio. Indeed, some writing guides of this kind go out of their way to advise candidates to avoid this choice. For, despite being the only folio genre free of word limits, poetry is no easy option. It is, rather, one of the more tricky and risky choices for several reasons.

While it is relatively straightforward for examiners to follow the marking criteria for a personal reflective essay or a persuasive essay, it is much more problematic for them – or anyone else for that matter – to determine what constitutes a successful poem. Libraries of books have been written on the definition of poetry – and few of them agree with each other. One of the most persuasive definitions is the idea that 'poetry is verse plus magic'. Now, while verse may be mastered with practice, magic is much harder to conjure up, especially in a way that pleases an unknown marker. He or she will, of course, follow strict marking criteria, but this is an area where subjectivity is almost impossible to banish entirely. Candidates be warned!

The safest advice here is to avoid this folio option unless you are someone who has been writing poetry for some time and is acknowledged as having talent in this area by critics whom you respect.

However, should you wish to pursue the poetry option, we are here to support you as much as we possibly can. On the following pages you will find some practical suggestions that respect certain criteria familiar to you already from other language outcomes for Higher/Intermediate 2.

- **Content:** Your poem should deal with material in a way that reveals depth and complexity of thought and sustained development. Your ideas should be relevant and appropriate for your purpose and audience. Think of the powerful poems you have studied in class; all of them respected these aims, exploring some complex aspect of the human condition with depth and sensitivity. Creating a poem is no easy exercise in superficial rhyming!
- **Structure:** Whether you opt for a traditional poetic form or free verse, you should remember that good poetry, like all good writing, respects structure. Sometimes, the structure is fairly obvious, as in traditional forms (such as the sonnet); sometimes it is less obvious in so-called free verse which, despite its name, is far from free and is often rigorously controlled by some structuring device of the poet's own invention. Such organisation, obvious or discreet, is necessary if your writing is to have impact.
- **Expression:** Of all the genres you may attempt for the folio, poetry is perhaps the one that is the most demanding in attention to expression. Here you need to deploy all your understanding of the poetic techniques and devices you have been studying over the years. To present your topic in a striking and original way you need to ensure your language has a novelty and richness that captures the reader's imagination. It is not merely chopped-up prose; its use of language should be heightened in some way, either by original choices of words, phrases and images or by unusual arrangements and patterning of words. Its ideas should be concisely expressed, with its sounds and rhythms helping to recreate for the reader the experience being described.
- **Technical accuracy:** This is a tricky one, for you will probably have already come across distinguished poets who dispense with traditional use of punctuation and capital letters! Poets allow themselves a certain flexibility in this area, but should you be tempted to experiment here,

remember that the end result must be intelligible to your reader – who in this case is also an examiner! You owe it to your work that it should be understood and appreciated; liberties with traditional grammar, syntax and punctuation should not be at the expense of intelligibility. It's the poetic equivalent of mumbling!

What should I write about?

Here, too, there are parallels with your other writing. Poetry is perhaps the most personal form of writing you can tackle. What works well in personal reflective writing also works well in poetry; drawing on your own experiences and feelings is the surest way of approaching a task of this kind. Poems that move readers need to carry the ring of conviction and the surest way of achieving this is to explore your own most powerful experiences and emotions. Detail here, too, is the best way of illuminating those emotions, with careful harnessing of word choice, figurative language, rhythm, alliteration, onomatopoeia, assonance and all the other devices available to poets.

Remember that you have the choice of a single poem or a set of thematically linked poems. Were you to take the latter approach, you will need to consider the subject of your linked poems at this early stage. What exactly will your theme be and will it be strong enough to sustain varied exploration over a set of poems?

Top Tip

Limit yourself to what you REALLY know about as subject matter. Professional writers can obviously imagine themselves into other people's situations and emotions, but at this stage in your development you may risk overstretching yourself.

What form should my writing take?

In a guide of this kind there is simply insufficient space to explore all the poetic forms on which you could draw. The fact that you are considering poetry at all suggests that you probably read quite a lot on your own, so may already be familiar with the more common forms:

Ballad Sonnet elegy ODE Haiku free verse dramatic monologue

Of course, you may not be considering a traditional form at all and may be contemplating free verse. We shall look at both but, before making any final choice, why not draft out very roughly part of your first ideas in a traditional form *and* free verse? Then decide on the basis of which one seems to be working out most successfully for you.

Top Tip

At this early stage try out in rough your initial ideas in both a formal structure and a free verse draft. Ask someone whose judgement you respect to look at them both and invite comments on what seems most effective for the topic in question. Your final choice has to be a personal one, but it often helps to hear other people's opinions.

Working in sonnet form

One traditional form that provides a satisfying structure and guides and shapes the deployment of ideas is the sonnet.

The sonnet has a long history from its origins in thirteenth century Italy. Basically, it is a fourteen line poem of ten syllables to a line. Over the centuries various forms of the sonnet have evolved. Two of the most common are the so-called Shakespearian (or English) sonnet which has three verses of four lines (a **quatrain**) followed by two final lines (a **couplet**) which rhyme and encapsulate the writer's 'message' for the poem, and the Petrarchan (or Italian) sonnet which is constructed around an **octave** (eight lines) followed by a second section of six (the **sestet**).

Each line follows the rhythmic pattern of an iambic pentameter. This sounds formidable but really only means that it has five 'bars' of iambs in each line, a rhythm based on one weak beat followed by a stronger one in each 'bar'. We see this rhythm at work in the opening line of Shakespeare's sonnet 12:

When I do count the clock that tells the time,

Here is the rest of this sonnet with its rhyme scheme marked beside it. Note that it follows the abab cdcd efef gg rhyme format.

SONNET 12

```
 u  /  u  /  u  /  u /  u  /
```
When I do count the clock that tells the time,   a
And see the brave day sunk in hideous night;   b
When I behold the violet past prime,   a
And sable curls all silver'd o'er with white;   b
When lofty trees I see barren of leaves   c
Which erst from heat did canopy the herd,   d
And summer's green all girded up in sheaves   c
Borne on the bier with white and bristly beard,   d
Then of thy beauty do I question make,   e
That thou among the wastes of time must go,   f
Since sweets and beauties do themselves forsake   e
And die as fast as they see others grow;   f
   And nothing 'gainst Time's scythe can make defence   g
   Save breed, to brave him when he takes thee hence.   g

Here we see Shakespeare examining the problems of ageing in the first twelve lines and offering in the final two the only solution he sees to combat it. It is addressed to a young man to whom he offers the advice that the only way to defeat time is to have a child and so perpetuate himself when he finally succumbs to death.

How do structure and meaning go together here? Let's look at how Shakespeare shapes his poem to bring out this central thought.

QUATRAIN 1 AND 2	Multiple examples of the depressing effects of the passing of time are given: bright day turns to gloomy night; violets wither; hair grows white; trees lose their leaves; crops are gathered in and borne off like a coffin in a funeral procession. Notice how this strong build-up of evidence is emphasised by the repetition of 'When ...' three times.
QUATRAIN 3	After the build-up of this evidential catalogue of the effect of time on nature in general, there comes a 'turn' on the word 'Then'. Now Shakespeare turns to the person to whom the sonnet is addressed. Armed with the 'evidence' he has already supplied about the corrupting effects of time, he suggests that this young man is no exception to this natural process and he, too, like other natural phenomena will lose his beauty and succumb to natural decay.
COUPLET	Having established that ageing is a natural process and that his handsome friend is no exception, Shakespeare appears to offer a solution: have a child and your offspring will perpetuate your image. In this way, you cheat death. Notice how the harvesting image in the couplet picks up the idea of the harvest field at the end of quatrain 2.

Here we have a perfect marriage of structure and meaning. Shakespeare uses the *shape* of the sonnet to mark three distinct stages in his *thought* process.

The first eight lines are devoted to the effects of time whose inevitability is emphasised by the relentless repetition of the word 'When', as if time were some kind of determined stalker. Then, having established his case, Shakespeare uses the next four lines to address directly his listener in a curious mixture of flattery and warning, before, in the final couplet, offering his escape from the problem.

Underpinning the inevitability of nature's decay is the rhyme scheme itself whose regularly recurring end-rhymes have their own kind of inevitability. The regular beat of the iambic pentameters assist this suggestion of the relentless forward march of time. Note, too, how Shakespeare ends the couplet on the extension of the harvesting image he had used earlier in the sonnet. Just as crops are harvested, so, too, are men.

In only fourteen lines we have a concisely conceived poem which takes a simple but disturbing idea – the destructive passing of time on man and nature – and uses formal structure, rhythm, rhyme and imagery to bring alive this central idea.

Here we have content, structure and expression working together to produce a satisfying unity.

Now, while there is no suggestion that you are expected to turn yourself into another Shakespeare, the application of similar techniques can help weld together your ideas into a form that readers can appreciate and identify readily.

The sonnet in Scotland

The sonnet as a poetic form has a long and distinguished history in Scotland. Alexander Montgomerie in the sixteenth century was delighting the court of James VI with his own variations on the Petrarchan sonnet (octave followed by sestet). In the twentieth and twenty-first centuries poets such as Robert Garioch, Edwin Morgan and Don Paterson have also turned to the sonnet form, often adopting, yet adapting, the Petrarchan rhyme scheme, like Montgomerie before them, to suit their own purposes.

We saw in the Shakespearian sonnet how ideas and form reinforced each other. This happens also in the Petrarchan sonnet where the octave may put forward a situation, an argument or idea and the sestet comments or focuses on it in some way.

Here is that structure at work in Edwin Morgan's Glasgow Sonnet No. 1. Note the Petrarchan sonnet rhyme scheme to which Morgan chooses to adhere strictly: abba abba cd cd cd

GLASGOW SONNET NO. 1

A mean wind wanders through the backcourt trash.	a
Hackles on puddles rise, old mattresses	b
puff briefly and subside. Play-fortresses	b
of bricks and bric-a-brac spill out some ash.	a
Four storeys have no windows left to smash,	a
but the fifth a chipped sill buttresses	b
mother and daughter the last mistresses	b
of that block condemned to stand, not crash.	a
Around them the cracks deepen, the rats crawl.	c
The kettle whimpers on a crazy hob.	d
Roses of mould grow from ceiling to wall.	c
The man lies late since he has lost his job,	d
smokes on one elbow, letting his coughs fall	c
thinly into an air too poor to rob.	d

(Collected Poems. Carcanet Press 1990)

OCTAVE QUATRAIN 1	Note how Morgan begins with a broad focus on the area, concentrating on a general panorama of desolation as the wind blows through the partly demolished site.
QUATRAIN 2	His camera moves into the crumbling five storey tenement, arriving at the fifth floor and the two 'mistresses' of the one remaining block.
SESTET	Focus narrows to illustrate the squalor of their flat, moving eventually into the bedroom where the ill, unemployed father lies coughing. The description has moved steadily from a wide exterior angle to a close-up of this figure of despair, coughing out his life. With the final references to 'air' the sonnet has come full circle, having begun noting the 'mean wind' in the back court. It began with a scene of urban desolation and ends with one of human desolation.

The thought process Morgan is following here, as in the Shakespeare sonnet, advances within the structural framework of the sonnet. The structure draws us gradually in, depositing us eventually at the bedside of the ill, unemployed man, having guided us to this point by exploring with an ever-narrowing lens the area and tenement block in question. Man and environment seem to share the same hopeless state, ruins of their past lives. The sonnet structure has played an important role in guiding us to this point.

Notice how in the Shakespeare sonnet the rhyme was highly noticeable to the ear. In the Morgan sonnet, on the other hand, the rhyme is often concealed by the sense running on to the next line and not always coming to a halt at the end of each line. This use of enjambment may appeal to writers (and readers) who prefer rhyme to be discreet rather than too obvious.

But whatever style appeals to you, note that the sonnet, despite its great age, is alive and highly effective in capturing and containing ideas concisely. It can comment on today's social world just as well as it could give advice to young noblemen in the sixteenth century.

Top Tip

Don't write off the sonnet as an old-fashioned vehicle for your ideas. It is not so much a straitjacket as a platform for helping you shape up your ideas. It is a form which allows you in only fourteen lines to demonstrate mastery of content, structure and expression. And where have we heard mention of these three criteria before?

Quick Task

Your school or local library is almost certain to have a copy of Shakespeare's sonnets and *Sonnets from Scotland* by Edwin Morgan. Browse through them to explore the vast range of topics for which each man has found the sonnet a useful vehicle. Note the variety Morgan at times brings to his rhyme schemes (particularly in the sestet), suggesting that there is room for considerable flexibility in what may look like a strict form.

Free verse

Do not be misled by the word 'free'. While free verse may be unshackled from the need for regular rhythms (such as the iambic pentameter we have noted in the sonnet) and the regularity of rhyme (which we have also seen at work in the sonnet), it is far from being an undisciplined form despite its apparent spontaneity.

Successful poets working in free verse have their own discipline to give shape to their ideas. They may have dispensed with fixed patterns of rhyme and rhythm but in their stead they employ a variety of different poetic techniques such as alliteration, assonance, imagery, repetition, personification, caesura and enjambment, the latter often in an attempt to capture the rhythms of everyday speech. In other words, they are using the techniques you have been encountering in your school or college study of poetry texts and textual analysis work for some time now.

If you are thinking of adopting this approach to writing your poem(s), you may already be well acquainted with masters of this form. Even so, it might be an excellent idea to see how it is being used currently by looking at the most recent, published poets. Go to the Scottish Poetry Library website as a useful starting point.

Top Tip

Click on spl.org.uk and you will find a wealth of information about poetry today. If you click on the spl.org.uk/poetry online option and then click on the anthology entitled Best Scottish Poems, you will be offered the annual anthologies since 2004. A gold mine of ideas and approaches!

Working in free verse

Let's look at how one poet shapes his thoughts and ideas in free verse. Here is a poem entitled 'The Blues' by Alan Riach.

THE BLUES
The lights are on all over Hamilton.
The sky is dark, blue
as a stained-glass window in an unfrequented church
say, by Chagall, with grand and glorious chinks
of pinks and purples,
glittering jewels on those glass-fronted buildings
where the lifts are all descending
and the doors are
being closed.
You're out there somewhere,
going to a concert in wide company or maybe
sitting somewhere weaving a carpet
like a giant tapestry, coloured grey,
pale brown, weaving the wool
back in at the edges of the frame, your
fingers deft as they turn the wool in tight and
gentle curves.

Or somewhere else.
What do I do
except imagine you?
The river I keep crossing
keeps going north. The trains
in the night cross it too.
Their silver carriages are blue.

(Originally published in *This Folding Map* (Auckland University Press 1991) but found in *Crossing Borders* published by the ASLS in 2008.)

Here the poet writes of 'the blues' he suffers being separated from the woman he loves. At first sight it may appear like a spontaneous outpouring of his emotion but, on closer inspection, we see that the poet has carefully constructed a framework of colours and images to give external form to his inner feelings.

Let's examine more closely how Riach uses various poetic techniques to shape his thoughts and emotions.

TECHNIQUE	EXAMPLE	EFFECT
Running throughout the poem is **a network of colour** references which go far beyond 'the blues' of the title. They help give a unifying shape to the poem as a whole.	*Blue, pinks, purples, grey, brown, silver* and finally *blue* again, rounding off the poem with the colour with which it began.	While blue is associated with sadness, note that this sadness is shot through with some warmer, brighter colours, hinting perhaps that this longing for the woman is a bitter-sweet sensation and not wholly negative.
Skilful use of **imagery** helps structure the poem's first half. The elaborate extended **simile** of the sun setting on glass-fronted buildings creates a glorious image of blues, pinks and purples all combined.	*Blue/as a stained-glass window ... by Chagall, with grand and glorious chinks/of pinks and purples,/ glittering jewels on those glass-fronted buildings/where the lifts are all descending/and the doors are/ being closed.*	The melancholy of 'the blues' is lightened temporarily by the sheer beauty of the 'glittering jewels' but the descending lifts and the closing doors return us to the idea of lowering spirits and exclusion/ separation.
In stark **contrast** to this extravagant outburst of exterior colour in the elaborate simile is the simple language as the poet imagines the woman in her evening's activities.	*Out there somewhere,/going to a concert in wide company* or perhaps *weaving a carpet.* Note, too, the more sober colours of grey and pale brown in contrast to the blues, pinks and purples.	Note the turn from external brilliance to interior tranquillity. From flamboyant imagery to intimately observed detail of the woman as she works. The striking contrast suggests both the extrovert glory and the inner quietness of a deep emotion.
Enjambment is used extensively to describe both the sunset and the woman at work.	Lines 2–9 and Lines 10–17	The poet's mastery of imagery and description is rendered unobtrusive by couching it in language which seems to capture the spontaneous flow of conversational speech.
Alliteration helps quietly in the overall picture-painting in the poem.	*grand and glorious, pinks and purples, weaving the wool*	These are small but significant brush strokes in the two major descriptive scenes that occupy the bulk of the poem.
The calculated **change of pace** brought about by the understated but slightly ominous comment in line 18.	*Or somewhere else.* Could it be that she is not just somewhere else but *with* someone else?	This thought seems to unsettle the poem's earlier poise. There is a new, nervy, quickened pace, created by the shortening of the lines which now employ rhyme for the first time. It is perhaps no coincidence that two of the rhymes fall on the key words 'you' and 'blue'.

Here, by a series of poetic devices which, unlike regular rhythm and rhyme, do not draw attention to themselves, Riach subtly externalises his inner feelings, linking them to a number of exterior images connected by a network of colour. By inviting the reader to witness and experience in words this carefully constructed external and internal landscape, Riach is offering much more than a beautifully observed panorama of the New Zealand city of Hamilton at twilight; he is inviting the reader to experience the unfolding of various states of mind and emotion as he contemplates 'the blues' brought on by the absence of the woman. His art here, however, is to conceal the craftsmanship whereby this insight is offered.

Here we see just a few of the methods available to the poet who chooses the free verse approach.

PROSPECTING IN PARTICK

It wasn't the dipping flight
of some departing finch,
not an indeterminate trill
from a wee silhouette on a treetop,
not a flash of olive and acid yellow
that might have been a greenfinch:

it was right here in White Street
on the pavement at St Peter's
exotic with its scarlet mask,
white cheeks and black cap.
Its eyes were shut, its head slack,
the black, white and gold wings folded.

I laid it in state under the fence
at number 48 and paid my respects
over the weeks as the mites
that burrow and chew spirited it away
leaving, as relics of treasure in Partick,
a tiny gold pinion or two.

Valerie Thornton

(*In the Event of Fire: New Writing Scotland 27.* ASLS 2009)

Quick Task

Should you be contemplating this approach, make sure you explore the methods and styles of just some of the published work available from the Scottish Poetry Library website. Alternatively, examine the following poems. Decide what structuring devices the poets have chosen. Could any of them be useful to you? List the ones you notice at work. Have they retained any structuring devices from more traditional poetry?

TIMETABLE

We all remember school, of course:
the lino warming, shoe bag smell, expanse
of polished floor. It's where we learned
to wait: hot cheeked in class, dreaming,
bored, for cheesy milk, for noisy now.
We learned to count, to rule off days,
and pattern time in coloured squares:
purple English, dark green Maths.

We hear the bells, sometimes,
for years, the squeal and crack
of chalk on black. We walk, don't run,
in awkward pairs, hoping for the open door,
a foreign teacher, fire drill. And love
is long aertex summers, tennis sweat,
and somewhere, someone singing flat.
The art room, empty full of light.

Kate Clanchy

(*Slattern.* Chatto and Windus/Macmillan 1995)

SEAGULL

We are the dawn marauders.
We prey on pizza. We kill kebabs.
We mug thrushes for bread crusts
with a snap of our big bent beaks.
We drum the worms from the ground
with the stamp of our wide webbed feet.
We spread out, cover the area –
like cops looking for the body
of a murdered fish-supper.
Here we go with our hooligan yells
loud with gluttony, sharp with starvation.
Here we go bungee-jumping on the wind,
charging from the cold sea of our birth.
Our flags are black, white and grey.
Our wing-stripes are our rank.
No sun can match the brazen
colour of our mad yellow eyes.
We are the seagulls.
We are the people.

Brian McCabe

(*Body Parts.* Canongate 1999)

The scriptwriting option

Like writing poetry, writing a script is a specialised undertaking. You need to ask yourself, therefore, if you wish to embark on learning how to produce a script when preparing a folio for an important public exam. You may, of course, have experimented in this genre previously and be familiar with aspects of it from an English, Drama or Media Studies course. If so, you may, after consultation with your teacher, decide to prepare a piece in this genre for the folio. Should this be the case, what follows will help you to face up to the technicalities of this challenge.

Links with prose fiction

You have the choice here of writing a scene, a monologue or a sketch. Whichever one you choose, however, the very first thing you must do is go back and read the section in this guide on prose fiction. For what makes for successful prose fiction is also the basis for successful scriptwriting. True, there are some very important differences, but in their need for sympathetic characters, convincing setting and persuasive plot, they have much in common. What do we mean by that, exactly? Let's take a look.

Creating characters

Show, don't tell

Apart from a few brief words of description in the stage directions before they enter, your characters depend entirely on what they say and do to come across as real people to the audience. And what they say and do is entirely up to *you*, as in prose fiction. (Look at the quick task on page 15 to remind yourself of how actions can illustrate character.)

In this scene from Rona Munro's *Bold Girls* we meet Cassie and Marie sitting on the ground outside a nightclub in the moonlight, watching the sky.

Top Tip

Contrasting characters give rise to conflict. Conflict between characters will keep your script moving briskly.

MARIE	This is ruining my good dress, Cassie.
CASSIE	It is not.
MARIE	It is so. I can feel the damp through the back of it.
CASSIE	That is not ruining your best dress.
MARIE	So you know what my bum's feeling better than I do?
CASSIE	You are ruining my best dress that you've had on loan since Easter.
MARIE	Oh – well I shouldn't think you'll want it back now.
CASSIE	(looking at the sky) Will you look at that.

(*Bold Girls*. Hodder & Stoughton 1991)

Here the author, very economically, signals quite a lot of information to us in eight lines. Cassie may be quite sharp-tongued but she is also fairly generous with her possessions, about which she seems not all that concerned. She seems more interested in relishing the beauty of the night. Marie, although rather absent-minded about her borrowings from her friend, is the more practically-minded of the two. She, unlike Cassie, is somewhat impatient with enjoying the pleasure of the moment, more concerned with the condition of the dress than admiring the beauty of the night. This short exchange underlines their personalities elsewhere in the play: one romantic, the other more practical.

Know them thoroughly

To know your characters well, you should think of constructing a table of biographic details similar to the one we created for characters in the short story on page 15. If your characters are not fully alive to you, you cannot expect the audience to believe in them.

Limit their number

Keep an eye on your word count. With limits of 1300 and 1000 words, you cannot afford too large a cast. As in a short story, a modest cast of characters is all you can manage if they are each to be fully characterised – and fully employed – in the scene.

Contrast them

Perhaps the best source of drama in any situation is contrasting characters, characters who are the opposite of each other in values, appearance, age or personality. A conflict in viewpoints is a sure way of keeping dialogue and plot on the move – and your audience interested.

Sourcing characters

You write best about what you know best. So maybe there are aspects of the characters of your friends or family which you could highlight? Perhaps there are characters from your reading that linger in your memory? By adapting personality traits from characters in fiction you have read about, or films you have seen, you can build up a convincing character of your own creation.

Tom Stoppard, in his play *Rosencrantz and Guildenstern are Dead,* examined the private lives of two minor characters who appear in Shakespeare's *Hamlet.* Think of a drama you may have been reading or watching. Is there a character whose off-scene life might be worth exploring?

Managing change

If your scene is to be complete in itself, it would be satisfying for the audience to see some development in the situation or in one or more of your characters in the course of your text. What actions or happenings are going to bring about this change credibly? Change in characters, to be convincing, needs to happen gradually.

Creating setting

Here, as much as in a short story, you need to consider the implications of whatever setting you choose for your script. You do not have the luxury of being able to describe it in great detail, other than in the stage directions at the start of the script. How are you to select a location and how is the audience to be given a sense of where they are?

Places of interaction

Avoid having your events taking place in a vacuum. The more convincing your setting, the more convincing your script. From your own experience, where do you see people meeting up with each other? Even in a school, you have various choices: a locker-room where people come in and out at will; a classroom where characters are constrained to be in the same place for a certain time; a library where conversation cannot be as open as it might be elsewhere. The setting in each case has an effect on how characters behave and talk.

Always target a setting in your mind's eye: the changing room in a gym, the lounge in an airport, a queue waiting for the opening of a sale in a store, and the waiting room in a medical centre are just some of the places where people meet and interact. A location or situation where people meet under some stress or tension can also realise fruitful results.

Respect the location

Once you have decided on your setting, don't ignore it. Settings have their own language, so use it. If a scene is taking place in the changing room of a gym, you will need to include remarks that remind us of this as keeping control of the interaction between the characters. For example:

Character 1	*It's as I was saying, we need to...*
Character 2	*Will you look at the state of this shower!*
Character 1	*...make sure that we don't let him get away with anything like he did last time. He's more than likely to do the dirty on us if we give him the chance.*
Character 2	*Aaaah! This water is freezing. It's always the same in this damned place. OK, OK, it's easy to say keep an eye on him, but how do we do that? Eh?*

Top Tip

Think about how music may illustrate a mood, a situation or a personality in a scene. Ian Rankin does this to good effect in his Rebus novels. It works well in drama, too.

As well as concentrating on carrying forward the action in your scene, you should keep in mind how best to exploit the language of the setting to create a credible backdrop to your characters.

Quick Task

To help you get started, think up a list of three characters sourced from any of the three ways suggested above in 'sourcing characters' Beside each character's name list at least four adjectives to describe them and two actions that might illustrate his/her personality.

Consider settings you know well from your own experience. List the out-of-school ones that would be likely to give you opportunities for encounters to take place. List, also, who you would be likely to encounter there. How would location affect the conversation?

Constructing plot

Once more, the constraints of word limits suggest that you should not be too ambitious in the scope of your script. To be satisfying, your scene, like a short story, needs a beginning, a middle and an ending. You will need, therefore, to calculate carefully how much dialogue is to be allocated to each section. To help you do this, it might be an idea to write out – in simple prose format – what your script is to be about. This will help you work out how many characters you need, how they relate to each other, what events are to take place and how the situation is to be resolved. It will also help you pace the action appropriately.

Creating a framework

In constructing a short story, we referred to a classic short story structure:

Top Tip

Check out news items in local and national newspapers as useful starting points for plots for scenes. The stories from the law courts make particularly fruitful reading.

- **a settled situation** involving two or three figures;
- **a complication** brought about by a new element, perhaps the appearance of a new character or the arrival of a letter;
- **a rising tension** brought about by the changed situation;
- **a crisis** which results in **a turning point** in the fortunes of the characters; and
- **a change** in situation, relationship, understanding or viewpoint.

The good news is that a similar approach to constructing a scene will also work well. We see it operating successfully here in the opening scene of a play we have already looked at: *Bold Girls*. In this play Marie, Cassie and Cassie's mother, Nora, are three women struggling to get by in the troubles of Northern Ireland in the latter part of the twentieth century. The settled situation we first encounter is a domestic one involving the weekly washing.

NORA	Is that the last of them, Marie?
MARIE	Just the towels... Oh Nora, you didn't need to carry that over, wee Michael was coming to get them.
NORA	Och you're all right? These towels is it?
MARIE	That's them.
NORA	This'll need to be the last. I've a load of my own to get in.
MARIE	Oh here Nora, leave them then!
NORA	No, no, we're best all getting our wash done while it's dry. We'll wait long enough to see the sun again.

Here we have a **settled situation** which will shortly be **complicated** by the appearance of a mysterious young girl, Deirdre, taking shelter from a street disturbance. Her strange behaviour leads to a **rising tension** which reaches a **crisis** when she attacks the portrait of Marie's late husband, precipitating a **turning point** in the play when the three main characters are forced to **change** the way they have viewed their lives to date.

This format works well in short scenes as well as entire plays, creating a structure which offers the audience a satisfying, well-rounded dramatic experience.

Creating dialogue

Dialogue is the life-blood of your script: it brings your characters to life, it helps create your setting and it is what moves on the story. So you first need to consider carefully the characteristics of spoken language to ensure your dialogue has a ring of reality about it.

Spoken versus written language

Listen carefully to your friends and family when they are speaking and you will notice that for a lot of the time they don't use what your English teacher would call 'proper' sentences. Often, sentences will remain incomplete or fail to end logically. Often, there will be pauses or partial repeats of what has already been said.

I was wondering... Well, the thing is,... erm... I was wondering... could you give me a lift down town? But only if you're free, you know. I mean... I don't want to...

Now, in your script, you don't want to recreate totally the often muddled speech of everyday conversation, but you do want to give it the flavour of real people speaking. Too correct or too long and your sentences will have a stilted quality that will sound unconvincing to your audience and be difficult for actors to carry off successfully. Spoken sentences tend to be shorter and less tightly controlled than written ones, but every word and expression needs to be carefully considered if your scene's characters and setting are to come alive and the plot is to move smoothly forward.

Top Tip

Successful dialogue requires shorter sentences than prose. It does not always need to be delivered in complete sentences. Great!

Dialogue and character

Personality can be revealed in aspects of a character's speech patterns. For instance, over-reliance on the following features suggests quite a lot about your characters:

- commands (bossy)
- questions (insecure, puzzled)
- incomplete sentences (vague)
- overlong sentences (long-winded, boring)
- a series of short sentences (brisk, dynamic)

Top Tip

Dialogue needs to sound like real people talking. Always try out your dialogue by saying it aloud.

In considering the speech behaviour of your characters, do not overlook the usefulness of items such as the following to convey embarrassment, hesitation or indecision in characters:

- lexical fillers: *you know..., well, I mean..., the thing is...*
- non-lexical fillers: *erm..., uhm..., mm..., aha..., oh!*

Social interaction often makes use of what are called phatic expressions. These have little real meaning yet lubricate the wheels of conversation.

- *You wish! You're welcome! What's up? Great! OK? You don't say.*

Expressions like these, used in moderation, help bring to dialogue the natural ring of everyday speech.

Quick Task

Here is some hopelessly dull dialogue which, with its over-wordy sentences and over-formal expression, is far too 'correct' to convince. Working with a partner, re-word it in any way you like as long as the message remains the same and the result sounds like real-world dialogue.

JASON   *I was hoping that we could spend the evening at the cinema, if you are not already doing anything. I know that 'The Men Who Stare At Goats' is still playing at the Omni. My sister saw it last night and says it's quite amusing.*

BECCA   *Yes, why not? That seems a good idea. I have to go to a play practice from three fifteen to four fifteen but after that I have nothing in particular to do since the only essay I have to do is not due until next Thursday. I really enjoy George Clooney films.*

JASON   *That's settled then. Will I call round for you or will we meet up somewhere? It seems pointless for you to come to me since Windsor Street is almost at the cinema.*

BECCA   *Whatever you wish. I can be ready at any time after six, so perhaps we can find somewhere to eat before the film? I believe there is a new Chinese which has just opened across the road from the cinema. Perhaps we could go there?*

Now read *aloud* your version with your partner. Does it sound like real people your age talking? If not, where does it fall down? What do you still need to do?

Page layout

A script is potentially a performance document, so layout needs to be clear and uncluttered for the benefit of the actors.

- A separate title page giving both the title of the script and the author's name adds a certain professional touch to the presentation. This page could also carry the *dramatis personae*, i.e. a list of the characters appearing in the scene and a brief description of their role, e.g. *Dr Percy: Elspeth's English teacher.*
- The heading of the scene should carry the scene's title and briefly describe (in italics) the scene of the action, e.g.

PUBLISH AND BE DAMNED

A bus stop in Bishopbriggs. Late afternoon in summer. Present day

- Names of characters should be in capital letters and set close in to the left of the page. (In some plays you will see names are followed by a colon.) There should always be plenty of space between the name of the character and his/her lines, simply for ease of reading.
- For ease of reading, stage directions which occur outside a speech should be indented to line up with the actors' speeches. In this way nothing interrupts the actors' line of vision as they scan the script for their lines. There is no need to use brackets here but italics will help separate stage directions from the actors' lines.
- Stage directions which are linked to a certain speech should be in brackets. Putting them in italics avoids any confusion with the actors' lines, e.g.

CROFTER (*brightly*) Och aye!

On the page, all that looks something like this brief extract from *The Cheviot, the Stag and the Black, Black Oil* by John McGrath:

	Doorbell rings.
WIFE	Get your shoes on, that'll be the tourists from Rotherham, Yorks, and put some peat on top of that coal – they'll think we're no better than themselves.
CROFTER	Aye, aye, aye – go you and let them in...
WIFE	Put off that television and hunt for Jimmy Shand on the wireless. CROFTER *mimes this action.* Oh God, there's the Marvel milk on the table, and I told them we had our own cows – *Bell rings again.*

(The Cheviot, the Stag and the Black, Black Oil. Methuen Drama 1974)

Sketch

A sketch is normally a fairly light-hearted piece of theatre, often involving only two people, in which some aspect of human nature or everyday life is mocked. Humour, however, is highly subjective and attempting to sustain it over 1000 or 1300 words may be rather challenging.

The Cheviot, the Stag and the Black, Black Oil by John McGrath, although technically a play, features a series of sketches which successfully epitomise the genre. On the previous page we saw a fragment of one sketch involving a crofter and his wife.

Another involves Andy McChuckemup, a Glasgow property developer, and Lord Vat of Glenlivet, a mad young laird. (Note the satirical names, a hallmark of sketch-writing.) The latter is approached by McChuckemup to buy up his family estate for a motel development. Here is part of it:

LORD VAT	No amount of money could compensate for the disruption of the couthie way of life that has gone on here uninterrupted for yonks. Your Bantu – I mean your Highlander – is a dignified sort of chap, conservative to the core. From time immemorial, they have proved excellent servants – the gels in the kitchen, your sherps – I mean your stalker – marvellously sure footed on the hills, your ghillie wallah, tugging the forelock, doing up your flies – you won't find people like that anywhere else in the world. I wouldn't part with all this even if you were to offer me half a million pounds.
ANDY	A-ha. How does six hundred thousand suit you?
LORD VAT	My family have lived here for over a century; 800,000.
ANDY	You're getting a slice of the action, Your Honour – 650,000.
LORD VAT	I have my tenants to think of. Where will they go? 750,000.
ANDY	We'll be needing a few lasses for staff and that... 700,000 including the stately home.
LORD VAT	You're a hard man, Mr Chuckemup.
ANDY	Cash.
LORD VAT	Done. (Shake)

(*The Cheviot, the Stag and the Black, Black Oil. John McGrath.* Methuen Drama 1974)

The play offers several other sketch models, in which various characters are satirised as exploiters of Scotland's natural heritage. Although McGrath is a masterly writer in this area, humour is difficult for the non-professional to bring off successfully. So, again, unless you have worked in this medium before, other genres might serve you better in your folio.

Monologue

A monologue may be part of a play or a stand-alone speech by a single character.

This is perhaps the most challenging of the script options in that it demands all the structure-building skills of the short story married to the character presentation strategies of a play script.

For Alan Bennett, one of the contemporary masters of monologue writing, the main difference between a play and a monologue derives from the fact that in a play there are different points of view, in a monologue there is only one point of view, with the rest of the story – and the world – seen from that point of view. This taxes writing skills considerably, for a single voice has to carry the responsibility for creating a whole imagined world, one which is entirely credible to the audience.

There is no one definition of a successful monologue, but to hold the attention of its audience, a monologue should incorporate at least some of the following features, illustrated here from Alan Bennett's *Talking Heads 1*:

- **a convincing 'voice':** Speech patterns are the dominating force in creating identity in a monologue. (Read again the 'dialogue and character' section of this chapter about how certain sentence elements can suggest personality.) Here is Violet, a stroke victim, speaking in Bennett's 'Waiting for the Telegram': *What's her name came round today... her that helps me with the talking... (She thinks) ... name of a cricket bat, else a gas oven... Verity. She's a nice-looking lass but makes nowt of herself, a big jumper thing...* Here, the fragmented, ungrammatical speech mirrors the muddled state of the old lady; a Yorkshire accent, too, can be detected at one point as part of the characterisation process.

- **a varied texture:** Although there is only one voice addressing the audience, in a successful monologue the character may conjure up other characters and dialogue with them. Here is Lesley, a young actress in Bennett's 'Her Big Chance': *I'm still sitting there hours later when this other young fellow comes in. I said, 'Gunther?' He said, 'Nigel'. I said, 'We spoke on the phone.' He said, 'Yes, I'm about to commit suicide. I've just been told. You don't water-ski.' I said, 'Nigel. I could learn. I picked up the skateboard in five minutes.'* Notice how the characteristics of the spoken voice are again underlined: speech is reported by 'said', as we do in conversation and no attempt is made at varying the verb, as we would in a short story.

- **an intriguing opening:** *I shot a man last week. In the back. I miss it now, it was really interesting. Still, I'm not going to get depressed about it. You have to look to the future. To have something like that under your belt can be quite useful, you never know when you might be called on to repeat the experience.* What, we wonder, is going on here? We want to know more.

- **progressive revelations:** From a puzzling opening such as the above, the writer gradually reveals what is being discussed. (Out-of-work actress Lesley is describing a past role in a film.) Equally gradual is the manner in which Lesley lets us discover her personality as the monologue progresses, a feature common to many monologues.

- **a controlled structure:** Although characters may *appear* to be rambling on, there is a tightly controlling hand at work. By the end of the monologue, we have been taken on a journey of revelation; the main character, too, may often have seen his/her life change significantly. Again, we are reminded of the close parallels with a good short story, as a seemingly stable situation is often undermined by events leading, in stages, to a new reality.

- **parallel perspectives:** Although the monologue *presents* a single point of view, the audience may develop its own. For, as characters tell their story from their own perspective, we see that their perspective might not be the only one possible. In 'Soldiering On', for instance, Muriel, following the death of her wealthy husband, is gradually impoverished by her dishonest son.

She ends up in grim poverty, but at no time does she allow herself to see her son for what he is – but the audience certainly does; and does so from her own remarks. A good monologue, therefore, will often signal a message to the audience above the narrator's head. What we are being told by characters is the truth as they see it, but it is not perhaps the whole or only truth.

(References are to *Talking Heads 1*. Alan Bennett. BBC Books 1988)

This is a difficult genre to bring off successfully. It may look straightforward in some ways, but examiners here, as elsewhere, will be looking to be impressed by content, structure, expression and technical accuracy. Controlling all these successfully in this genre requires considerable skill (particularly structure), so make sure you have read plenty of them before you even consider this option. Alan Bennett's *Talking Heads* and the monologues in Liz Lochhead's *True Confessions and New Cliches* are useful starting points. In the latter, Lochhead offers fine models for anyone wishing to attempt a monologue in Scots.

The discursive family

Argumentative/persuasive: how do they differ?

- An argumentative essay is one in which you examine and evaluate objectively* opposing viewpoints on a controversial topic. The discussion, which should be conducted in formal and neutral language, will require research and evidence taken from authoritative sources. You may conclude by supporting one or other of the points of view or you may decide to retain your objectivity, suggesting, for instance, that there is still insufficient evidence to decide for one side or the other.

- A persuasive essay is one in which you are trying to convince the reader/examiner to accept your subjective** view on a particular topic. Here, too, soundly researched evidence is important but so is your ability to balance this with the language of persuasion to win over the reader/examiner. No balance of evidence is required as in an argumentative essay, but it would be intelligent to acknowledge the existence of a contrary view.

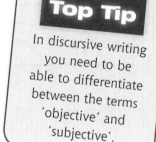

Top Tip

In discursive writing you need to be able to differentiate between the terms 'objective' and 'subjective'.

*__Objective:__ based on fact. *With an approval rating of only 22% according to a CBS News/New York Times poll, George W. Bush left office as the most unpopular departing president since records began 70 years ago.* Based on evidence, this comment counts as a legitimate statement.

**__Subjective:__ based on personal response. *Nobody had any time for George W. Bush when he left office. He was the worst American president ever.* Based only on emotion, this comment counts as a personal opinion.

Argumentative/persuasive: what do they share?

As we have seen above, the argumentative and the persuasive essay differ in their way of exploring an issue. What they share, however, are certain discursive family resemblances.

INTRODUCTION	This should capture the reader's attention and interest in your topic. This may take a variety of forms, but usually it should inform the reader about background to the topic, explaining why this subject is important and worthy of our attention. A persuasive essay will indicate the idea which you wish the reader to support. An argumentative one will lay out the two sides of the issue. The introduction may also indicate some kind of road map of the structure of the essay.
BODY PARAGRAPHS	Here you set out your ideas in a logical sequence, showing a clear line of development, with each step in your discussion/argument being made clear. Progression from one paragraph to the next should be smoothly signalled by connecting devices. One main point per paragraph is the most coherent way to advance your case.
CONCLUSION	This re-visits the main points of your essay, reminding the reader of the views expressed earlier. In summarising the main thrusts of your discussion you should look for fresh wording which does not simply repeat the vocabulary of your introduction. A good knowledge of synonyms helps here. On no account introduce new material. The reader should be left feeling the topic has been credibly and authoritatively explored.

Argumentative/persuasive: what tools do they use?

	ARGUMENTATIVE	PERSUASIVE	INTENDED EFFECT
Giving illustrative examples	*	*	To assist reader's understanding
Quoting/rebutting/criticising expert opinion	*	*	To show expertise in area of discussion
Using analogies (comparing this situation to another)	*	*	To point out parallels helpful to understanding
Using polls/surveys	*	*	To show viewpoint supported by research
Mentioning and responding to opposing views	*	*	To demonstrate skill in argument
Indicating consequences/ implications of 'for' and 'against' positions	*	*	To indicate ability to follow through arguments
Neutral language	*		To review information impartially
Emotive language		*	To appeal to reader's feelings
Rhetorical questions		*	To invite reader's agreement
Attitude markers (clearly, obviously, fortunately, surely, etc.)		*	To show commitment

Checking out persuasive writing

Editorials in national newspapers are prime examples of persuasive writing. With a partner, find examples in the text to match the discursive features in the table below.

A scheme of mice and men best laid aside

In what must rank as some of the most bizarre and useless animal research, scientists have determined that laboratory mice when in pain display human-like facial expressions. A 'mouse grimace scale' was constructed to measure pain based on five distinct 'pain faces'. The pious hope of the scientists is that the work will assist research and help prevent unnecessary suffering in mice. Surely the fact that they grimaced at all was evidence of pain? Not to say that the injection of pain-inducing substances such as acetic acid and mustard oil might just have given a clue that pain was being suffered.

It is hard to imagine research more likely to bring vehement protests from the ranks of anti-vivisectionists and campaigners against animal cruelty. Most of us accept the need for animal testing and research only reluctantly and on the strict proviso that such research has to be shown

Top Tip

Note that in this article, the writer was careful to alternate openly persuasive writing with writing that appeared to be more neutral. This makes sense. Be relentlessly persuasive and you may put readers off.

to be absolutely necessary. But were these experiments absolutely necessary? To the question: "How much would the human face react if the stomach was filled with acetic acid?" the answer is so glaringly obvious as not to require further experimentation. Are mice so different?

Trap a mouse in a cage, let in a cat and a facial grimace would soon become obvious. Trap a human, let in a lion and we would have other things to do than measure facial grimaces.

(*The Scotsman*, Monday 10 May 2010, p.28. Edited slightly)

Quoting/rebutting/criticising expert opinion	
Using analogies	
Emotive language	
Rhetorical questions	
Attitude marker	

Quick Task

Check out the editorial columns in a serious newspaper of your choice and see how many of the persuasive features noted above you can find. Are there any other devices which indicate the writer is seeking to bond with the reader?

Quick Task

Where would you be most likely to place the following remarks? Remember that while persuasive writing may make use of emotive language, there will be times when it, too, like argumentative writing, may want to present itself in formal, neutral language. Could some remarks perhaps fall into both columns?

	ARGUMENTATIVE	PERSUASIVE
What kind of government treats pensioners in this way?		
According to Professor Aitchison writing later in the same article, Hardwick's contribution was instrumental in securing in due course a change in the law.		
Imagine for a moment the sight of forty starving hounds pursuing one exhausted fox.		
According to Professor Aitchison writing later in the same article, Hardwick's astounding breakthrough saw the law changed virtually overnight.		
Such high-handed behaviour is more than a little reminiscent of some fascist regimes of the 1930s.		
This, while seen by many as revolutionary at the time, was later regarded as a somewhat tentative response to the situation.		
Who could remain silent in the face of such provocation?		
What we need now is not quick fixes and catchy sound bites but carefully considered research, based on good, old-fashioned principles of the kind that won Britain its world-wide reputation for state-of-the-art engineering.		
Close inspection reveals an unusual and disturbing trend in the figures, with more and more younger women appearing to be joining the ranks of medium to heavy smokers.		

Planning, researching, and plagiarism

Planning

Essays which succeed are essays which are planned. Examiners will tell you that structure is just as important as content. An essay that flows easily from point to point in a coherent way is one which convinces far more than one full of brilliant insights but chaotically put together.

Structure doesn't just happen; it has to be planned for. So how do you plan an essay?

- Start with a topic you think you may enjoy, even if you are not sure what you are going to say about it, or what approach you are going to take.
- Brainstorm as many points, positive or negative, as you can around it.

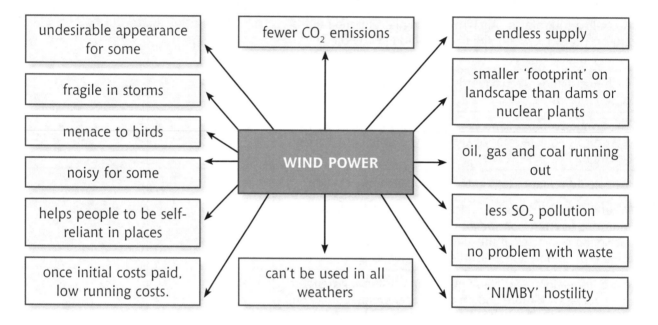

In this mind map form these points are rather confusing. Some points, even at this early stage, seem important, others less so. So let's see if we can sort them out into groups that belong together in some way.

This might lead us to the following groupings.

Fewer CO_2 emissions (global warming)	Oil, gas, coal running out	'NIMBY' hostility	Once initial costs over, low running costs
Less SO_2 pollution (acid rain)	Endless supply	Undesirable appearance for some	Helps people to be self-reliant
Smaller 'footprint'		Can't be used in all weathers	
No dams/nuclear plants		Menace to birds	
No waste problems			

In other words, we end up with four groupings to which we might give the following four titles: Column 1: Environment, Column 2: Sustainability, Column 3: Reaction, Column 4: Cost.

So, here already are four possible sections to an essay. At this point we still may not know if we are writing an objective/argumentative essay or a subjective/persuasive one, but that we can leave until later. Now it is time to see if the points that have crossed our mind in this random way can stand up to some factual research.

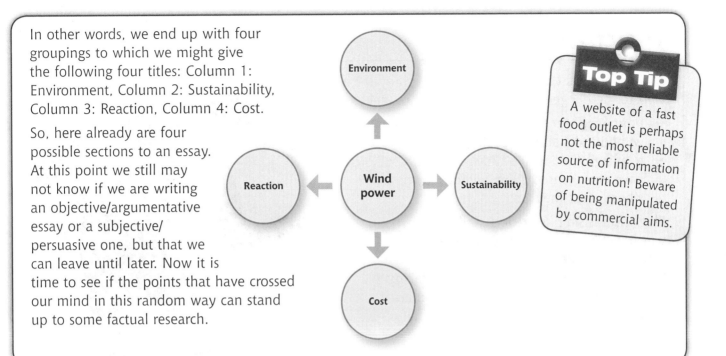

Top Tip

A website of a fast food outlet is perhaps not the most reliable source of information on nutrition! Beware of being manipulated by commercial aims.

Researching

A successful essay needs evidence. You may have some interesting ideas on your chosen topic, but now is the time to make sure your ideas can be supported by researched information. Take your ideas to a library and find out whether your thoughts are backed up by 'authority', i.e. evidence from expert opinion of some kind. This may take many forms:

Top Tip

When the time comes to write up your essay, make sure you acknowledge your source and the context from which the quotation emerged.

- Articles in quality newspapers. Insert key words into the paper's website. Ensure the information is the latest possible. Articles from magazines, trade publications and journals are also available from http://findarticles.com.
- Thematic studies across genres. Most school/college libraries have collections of studies on issues such as capital punishment and abortion.
- Biographies/autobiographies of relevant key figures.
- Pressure group handouts. But be alert to their bias.
- Essays/extracts from literary/ scientific/medical texts.
- Carefully selected websites.

Be careful in your selection of evidence, particularly if you use the internet. Ensure your evidence is as recent as possible. How impartial does it seem? Of course, you can show the examiner your ability to refute / counter-argue/dispute information if it appears to be faultily researched, poorly argued or plain biased.

Plagiarism

At this point, as you make your notes, you must be alert to the dangers of plagiarism. This can mean:

- borrowing text from recognised authorities without fully acknowledging its source
- relaying other people's ideas, even if you have paraphrased them, without saying whose ideas they are.

Plagiarism is simply intellectual theft which will be quickly noticed and severely dealt with. Sometimes, of course, this may happen unintentionally when you are taking notes, but it is something for which you are responsible and of which you must be fully aware.

Checking for plagiarism

Here is a brief extract from a study of Scottish architecture by Glendinning and MacKechnie.

> For much of the 20th century, Scottish architecture was dominated by violent reaction against the Victorian age: there was, for several decades, an almost complete shift towards a collective modern world of disciplined mass movements.

(Scottish Architecture, Miles Glendinning and Aonghus MacKechnie. Thames & Hudson World of Art)

Which student is guilty of plagiarism?

Student A

In their study of Scottish architecture Glendinning and MacKechnie see it as being 'dominated by violent reaction against the Victorian age' for much of the 20th century. They perceive an almost complete shift over many years towards the modern world of disciplined mass movements.

Student B

Twentieth century architecture, according to Glendinning and MacKechnie, shifted towards 'a collective world of disciplined mass movements' which they see as part of a violent reaction against the Victorian age. This reaction continued for several decades.

Student C

Glendinning and MacKechnie consider Scottish architecture as 'dominated by violent reaction against the Victorian age' for a large part of the twentieth century. They view this reaction as being coupled to 'an almost complete shift towards a collective world of mass movements'.

Student D

For several decades there was a shift in Scottish architecture towards a collective world of mass movements as part of a strong reaction against the Victorian age.

Top Tip

If you feel you might be guilty of plagiarism, even unintentionally, always write down your notes in your own words and write down quotations in inverted commas with their source beside them. Otherwise, you can waste hours looking for the source when you are writing up. A highlighter is also a good way to distinguish quotations in your notes.

Structuring and sequencing

Now that you have gathered together your information you have a decision to make.

Is your essay to be:

- an argumentative essay with your support finally awarded to one side of the debate?
- an argumentative essay where you withhold support for any one side in the debate?
- a persuasive essay in which you argue for a certain line of thought which has emerged from your research?

Top Tip

The examiner is more interested in how you put your case, than in what you believe.

The choice you make at this point will govern the structure and sequence of the essay you intend writing.

In an argumentative essay...

Let's look first at what you are setting out to achieve in your essay. Whatever your stance, you should aim for an effortless flow in the sequence of your ideas. There should be no jarring changes of direction to bewilder the reader. This will have a bearing on how you structure and sequence the information in your essay.

If you are planning to award your support *finally* to one side of the debate, a useful structure is this:

Introduction in which **both** viewpoints are set out
First paragraph with ideas **contrary** to your final viewpoint
Subsequent paragraphs with ideas **contrary** to your viewpoint
First paragraph with ideas **coinciding** with your final viewpoint
Subsequent paragraphs with ideas **coinciding** with your final viewpoint
Conclusion summing up and making your stance clear

Top Tip

In an argumentative essay make sure your arguments flow seamlessly into each other. Don't jerk the reader's concentration with unanticipated switches of direction.

This is a structure which makes for a seamless flow, for there is no need in your conclusion to jerk your reader away from the ideas you have been putting forward in the final stages of your essay. Your supportive conclusion follows on naturally from the case you have been making and it is much easier to take the reader with you. Should you finally back information which you gave much earlier in the essay, there could be an uncomfortable break in the reader's concentration as he/she reminds himself/herself what these earlier views were. Your conclusion, of course, should revisit these earlier points, but your final arguments will be fresher in readers' minds, thus making it easier for them to understand why you reached this position.

If you are planning to write an argumentative essay in which you intend to remain neutral, there is no similar need to sequence your information in this way. If, however, you choose this approach, make sure your reasons for standing back from supporting one or other side stand up to scrutiny and don't just show you to be a ditherer. Is there insufficient evidence to decide one side or the other? Is the situation changing in a way that makes a definitive decision now unwise? You need a convincing reason.

In a persuasive essay ...

Here you are unashamedly setting out to persuade readers to back the case you are putting forward, so you are freed from the necessity of putting forward a case as carefully balanced as in an argumentative essay. It is a wise writer, however, who makes it clear to readers that he/she has the intelligence to know there will be opposition to the case being advanced. It might be sensible, therefore, to concede and deal with some major point that might be levelled against your thesis. Some essay writing guides may tell you to acknowledge this alternative viewpoint before your conclusion. On reflection, however, this might not be ideal, for surely you want that opposing view to be long forgotten as you sweep to your conclusion? You do not want hints of doubt appearing in your reader's mind so late in the essay. So an effective structure for a persuasive essay might be as follows:

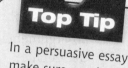

Top Tip

In a persuasive essay make sure you build to your strongest argument. A weak final argument will be an anti-climax and will weaken your case.

Introduction making stance clear
Acknowledgement yet rejection of alternative viewpoint
First persuasive paragraph
Subsequent persuasive paragraphs
Conclusion

Introductions

Introductions: the argumentative approach

There is no one way to begin a discursive essay. Here, however, is a fairly typical introduction to an essay taking the argumentative approach. (Although students in Scotland do not pay tuition fees, it is a topic that is widely discussed in student circles.) Note the moves the writer makes.

The case for and against raising university fees

historical context

In post-war welfare Britain there grew up generations of young people who looked on free university tuition as a norm. With escalating funding costs, however, and the need to keep British universities ahead in world academic league tables, the sustainability of free university education came to be questioned. In October 1998 the then Labour government introduced student tuition fees, set at the time at £1000 per year. Over the years the figure has been raised and currently stands at around £3000 on average. A recent University UK report which recommended that this figure be raised to £5000 found commentators sharply divided. University vice-chancellors and many politicians argued that increased fees were imperative to maintain standards and safeguard courses. Students and their leaders maintained that graduates left university with debts of £22 000 on average; a further rise would increase this indebtedness to £34 000. In seeking to determine the validity of the opposing stances, this study will look at the case for freezing any rise, the argument put forward by the universities and explore possible alternative funding mechanisms.

focus of controversy

viewpoint one

viewpoint two

essay's intentions / road map

Introductions: the persuasive approach

Now look at this introduction to an essay taking the persuasive approach. Note the moves the writer makes.

An increase too far: why university fees should not rise

historical context

In the heady days of post-war Britain, a fairer nation in terms of health care and education seemed not just possible but inevitable. Free university tuition, backed by local authority maintenance grants, was a central feature of the Labour government's education policy. At last, able young people from underprivileged backgrounds, cheated for generations of the chance to better themselves academically, could develop their talents in the way denied to their parents. For decades, tens of thousands of young people passed through Britain's universities, enriching immeasurably

topic's significance assessed

> **Top Tip**
>
> Keep a sharp eye on the word count of your essay. The maximum for Higher is 1300 words and for Intermediate 2 is 1000. So devoting 10–15% to your introduction seems reasonable.

the ranks of public service and private enterprise. In 1998, however, at a stroke, another Labour government introduced tuition fees of £1000 and replaced the grant system with student loans. Today, fees stand at around £3000 and the average student leaves university with crippling debts of around £22 000. Now, there is talk of fees rising to £5000 a year. Can this be fair? Let us look at why this rise is unacceptable and what can be done to halt the growth of this intolerable burden.

subjective reaction and essay's intentions/road map

focus of controversy

Quick Task

Check out both introductions above for the following points.

	ARGUMENTATIVE	PERSUASIVE
Neutral title	Yes/no	Yes/no
Emotive language	List	List
Neutral language	Yes/no	Yes/no
Rhetorical questions	Yes/no	Yes/no
Structural points in common	List	List
Structural differences	List	List

Quick Task

Using material from the above introductions on university fees and any of the following information which you think you may need, write the introduction to a persuasive essay in which you take the *opposite* point of view from the persuasive essay introduction above.

- Universities across the country, according to a *Guardian* report, are preparing to axe thousands of teaching jobs, close campuses and drop courses to cope with government funding cuts amounting to at least £950 million over the next three years. More reliance needs, therefore, to be placed on tuition fees.
- Professor Paul Wellings, vice-chancellor of Lancaster University, recently told a conference on higher education funding that charging higher fees was the only viable way to boost university finances.
- Some in government circles think that tuition fees should be doubled to fund an expansion of bursaries for poorer students.

Quick Task

- Working with a partner, choose one of the following topics.
  a. **Wind power as a source of energy**
  b. **Future of nuclear weapons in post cold war world**
  c. **Healthy eating in schools**
  d. **Separate schools for gifted children**
- Consider carefully the *wording* of your title; it should reflect the persuasive/argumentative nature of the text to come.
- Together, research briefly what you might include in an introduction.
- One partner should then write the introduction to an argumentative approach; the other should write the introduction to a persuasive approach to whatever topic you have chosen.
- When you have finished, compare the structure and language with the introductions above. Have you followed the formats suggested? Or have you had to alter them to accommodate the topic? Is your language (neutral/emotive) appropriate to the task? Is your word count about right?

The discursive body paragraph

You may be relieved to hear that the body paragraphs in discursive essays, whether they are argumentative or discursive, can often follow a pattern you already know from your critical essays on literature: SEEC, i.e. a statement, followed by evidence which, in turn, is followed by an explanation of that evidence and finally a personal comment on all of that. Of course, we are not dealing with literature here, but our way of creating convincing paragraphs can be rather similar. Here is the SEEC format adapted to suit discursive writing.

STATEMENT	Here you set out the main point you wish to make in the paragraph that follows. Some people refer to this statement as the topic sentence, but remember your statement may require more than one sentence to express fully the topic to be discussed. It should be a fairly broad, general remark, with no detail given here.
	In recent years France has proved to be a leader in tackling the problem of child obesity. Research at the University of Grenoble suggests that there has been a reduction in cases being seen by family doctors.
EVIDENCE	Evidence can take multiple forms: it may come from statistics, information in a newspaper or journal article, comments by well-known experts in the subject, surveys, polls, an illustrative anecdote, personal experience. This section can usually be distinguished by the appearance of detailed information, quotations from a text or statistics.
	According to Professor Gerard Dalle writing in ...
EXPLANATION	This is where you help the reader understand the implications of the evidence which you have just produced.
	From statistics such as these, it is clear that ...
	Should you wish to rebut or question certain evidence, this is where you would do so.
COMMENT	Here you sum up the significance/implications of the information gleaned from the paragraph, perhaps including a link to the next paragraph if at all possible.
	But while the problem of child obesity may be being tackled systematically in certain forward-thinking countries in Europe, there is no similar approach being developed in Scotland at the moment.

Quick Task

Here is an SEEC body paragraph for: a) an argumentative and b) a persuasive essay, dealing with the environmental benefits of wind power. The SEEC sequence order has been deliberately confused. Determine the correct order of the paragraphs, filling in the grid on the following page with the appropriate number. List the distinguishing characteristics which influenced your choice. Check what these are with the grid on page 59 and the grid on the previous page.

1. *According to the Renewable Energy Laboratory of America, the construction and installation of wind turbines, equipment and access roads takes up 5% of a wind farm site, leaving the rest free for existing farm usage. It is also claimed that CO_2 emissions could be reduced. General Electric suggests that in the course of a 20-year lifespan, a 100 MW wind farm has the capacity to generate the same amount of electricity as burning 2·9 million tons of coal or over 62 billion cubic feet of natural gas.*

5. *These are facts and figures which merit serious attention. From the point of view of productive land use and reduced atmospheric pollution, wind-powered electricity appears to offer significant benefits over more traditionally-sourced power. Of course, many such claims derive from sources which are biased in favour of wind power. Their claims, while attractive, must, therefore, be tempered with a certain caution.*

6. *In a world in which fossil fuels are increasingly blamed for harmful effects on the environment, it is hardly surprising that wind power is viewed favourably by many governments. As well as environmental benefits, there are also economic ones.*

4. *Among the several claims put forward by advocates of increased reliance on wind power is the beneficial effect which they maintain it would have on the environment.*

3. *So who could be against such an approach to power generation? Here is a method which is kind not just to the land but the air above it too, one which is sourced from a supply that is endless, a fact which makes it equally attractive from another point of view, the economic one.*

2. *Key among the various advantages which wind power brings is its beneficial effect on our environment. By more widespread use of it, we could prove ourselves to be much better custodians of our planet.*

7. *For a start, the construction and installation of a wind farm leaves a far smaller footprint than do other more polluting means of generating electricity. According to the respected National Renewable Energy Laboratory of America, wind turbines, equipment and access roads can take up a fairly insignificant 5% of the wind farm site, leaving the rest free for existing farm usage. Furthermore, the reduction in noxious, global-warming CO_2 emissions could be drastically reduced. Figures produced by General Electric suggest that in the course of a 20-year lifespan, a 100 MW wind farm has the capacity to generate the same amount of electricity as burning 2·9 million tons of coal or over 62 billion cubic feet of natural gas.*

8. *From facts and figures such as these it is clear that with the application of wind power we are in a favourable position to take much greater care of our already seriously damaged planet, victim of many years of indiscriminate use of polluting fossil fuels. And while not to every taste, wind turbines disturb the landscape far less than dams, coal mines and nuclear power plants with all their invasive satellite roads and buildings.*

	ARGUMENTATIVE	PERSUASIVE	DISTINGUISHING CHARACTERISTICS
Statement			
Evidence			
Explanation			
Comment			

Answer

	Argumentative	Persuasive
Statement	4	2
Evidence	1	7
Explanation	5	8
Comment	6	3

Argumentative/persuasive: the conclusion

Your conclusion marks your last point of contact with the examiner. You wish, therefore, to leave a good impression. You want him/her to feel that you have fully achieved what you undertook to do in the introduction: either to explore both sides of a controversial topic or to present persuasively a case about which you feel strongly. It should have the ringing finality that the final bars of good music have; it should not just stop, or worse still, limp to a halt.

So what does the examiner expect of a conclusion?

- It should briefly re-visit the main points/arguments made in your discussion. If you decide to support one side of the debate, you need to make it clear why this choice has been made. You should try to vary your vocabulary somewhat here, employing synonyms wherever possible to give a freshness to your comments rather than recycling the same phrases you may have used earlier.

- It should be made clear *why* this topic has been an important one for you to have been discussing at such length. What bearing does it have on the world today or tomorrow? On human happiness? On the kind of society we have made for ourselves?

- It should NOT introduce any specifically new material at this stage.

- It is an elegant point of style if you can manage to refer back in your conclusion to some remark you made or question you raised right at the beginning. This signals your essay has come – satisfyingly – full circle.

- It is academic practice to acknowledge where your principal sources came from. See the 'report writing' chapter for full details of how this list of references might be laid out (bibliographical referencing section on pages 69–70).

How well am I arguing my case?

Earlier (page 47) we looked at some of the discursive tools you as a writer might use to put forward information and views. But once we have appreciated the importance of neutral versus emotive language, the usefulness of analogies/examples, the appropriateness of rhetorical questions and all the other devices we noted, there is still the matter of how you present yourself and your information.

Qualifying strength of claim

In both argumentative and persuasive essays you need to establish yourself in the reader's eyes as a good judge of material. Even in a persuasive essay, where are you aiming to influence the reader's opinion, you need a measure of caution. You wish to be seen as someone who has researched the subject well, reflected thoughtfully on the evidence and is now putting forward a considered case. Beware, then, of making table-thumping categorical statements like: *This proves conclusively ...* or *This definitely shows ...* You may come across as crudely opinionated and may irritate your reader. And an irritated reader is unlikely to be a convinced reader. Be confident, but sensitively so. Ways of keeping a reader onside are:

Learn to moderate claims by measuring probability.

Are you suggesting that a certain action *will result in ..., may result in ..., could result in ...* a particular outcome? And how likely is it to happen? Is its likelihood *very probable, probable, possible, conceivable, unlikely, highly unlikely*? Is there *a strong possibility, a good possibility, a definite possibility, a slight possibility, a remote possibility, only a remote possibility* that this action *will/may/could* be effective?

Consider distancing yourself from a claim.

What is the effect on your reader of suggesting *wind power has certain advantages*, rather than *wind power seems to have more advantages* or even *it would appear/seem that wind power has more advantages*?

Qualify the evidence if necessary.

Given that the data is still only limited ..., On the data currently available ..., Accepting that existing data is difficult to verify fully as yet ..., Based on what evidence currently exists ... This shows you have examined the evidence as it exists but are exercising caution in coming to a judgement.

Qualify whatever/whoever it is you are talking about.

Some/many/certain drivers find that ..., A minority/majority/number of drivers claim that ..., In certain parts of the world, drivers are known to ..., Drivers in lower income brackets claim that ..., In a number of cases, drivers report that ...

Select vocabulary carefully.

Compare *Raising fees <u>causes</u> fewer students to apply to ...* with *Raising fees <u>contributes to</u> fewer students applying to ...* And, of course, you can add *will/may/could* to such verbs to shade your judgement even more. To say nothing of *probably, possibly, conceivably* which are words which add extra qualifications.

But be careful. Over-qualifications are just as dangerous to your reputation as a judge of evidence as sweeping generalisations. There is the danger of sounding *too* tentative. You must learn to strike the correct balance.

Checking for sensible qualifications

Work on these sweeping generalisations and make them respectable claims which reflect well on you as a judge of information. Get a partner to check the end result to see if you are making balanced, defensible claims which you could follow up with convincing evidence.

- Eating sweets causes obesity.
- Regular revision is the best way to achieve academic success.
- Physical exercise leads to happiness.
- Japanese cars are more reliable than German ones.
- Nuclear power is a better source of electricity than wind power.

Top Tip

Don't *bully* your readers into your viewpoint; *lead* them in with carefully qualified statements which show you to be a thoughtful judge of evidence. Avoid thumping the table!

Arguing intelligently

Avoid a non sequitur.

A non sequitur (Latin for *it does not follow*) is a conclusion that does not logically follow the evidence. For example, *Pensioners' leaders have been critical of the general treatment handed out to old people by various governments over the past few decades, suggesting that the pensioners' winter heating allowance has been a waste of money.* These two statements do not follow. Criticism of a number of measures does not mean that all measures are unappreciated.

Avoid false authorities.

A professor of dietetics is an appropriate authority on nutrition; a television celebrity is not, unless, of course, he or she is known to have specialised knowledge.

Avoid the over-simplification of the false dilemma.

This is to assume there are only two possible options when in fact there are more. *Either we choose wind power or we see carbon emissions inexorably rise.* There are other power sources which are carbon neutral.

Avoid outdated information.

In our multimedia age there is no excuse for arguing from statistics that are not current.

Avoid false analogies.

This is when you claim two situations are alike when they are not. *We have laws to assure the purity of our food; why can't we have the same thing to clean up television?* While purity in food terms is measurable and objective, purity in entertainment terms is a matter of subjective opinion. Be careful in the use of analogies: they are best used to help a reader understand a concept or position; they do not really prove anything.

The final checklist

When we become deeply involved in our writing, we can sometimes overlook its faults. Before handing in either draft, look through it quite ruthlessly with this checklist beside you.

FOR AN ARGUMENTATIVE DRAFT	FOR A PERSUASIVE DRAFT
1. How well is the case balanced? Is there sufficient evidence presented on both sides?	1. How well is the case presented? Would a reader feel inclined to move his/her position after reading?
2. If I settle for one side of the argument, are the arguments for doing so convincing? If I do not, is the reason for neutrality convincing?	2. What might persuade the reader here? The force of the evidence or the style of arguing? Are either weak, in your opinion?
3. Does the introduction tell the reader everything that needs to be known? Is there too much or too little scene setting?	3. Does the introduction set out everything that needs to be said? Is my stance credible and set out sensibly in this section?
4. Where do I feel the essay is strongest? Why do I think this is so?	4. Where do I feel the essay is strongest? Why do I think this is so?
5. How well do I think the essay is organised? Be honest! Does it flow?	5. How well do I think the essay is organised? Be honest! Does it flow?
6. How do I think the essay could be improved? More evidence? Better expression of the arguments?	6. What might I do to improve the essay? More evidence? More persuasive arguing?

How do reports fit into the discursive family?

Should you opt for this folio choice, the good news is you will find many of the skills required for writing discursive essays will again prove useful. Admittedly, a report is very different from an essay in important ways, but there still remain family resemblances. Let's take a look at what some of them are before we look at the major differences.

RESEARCH TECHNIQUES	When researching information for your report, you must be careful to ensure that you can discriminate between subjective opinion and objective fact.
	To avoid the dangers of accidental plagiarism, notes should always be made in your own words and not the words of the source.
	Sources should also be checked as far as possible for independence of viewpoint.
	Note down the exact source of your information to save time searching for it should you require further details or for preparing a bibliography.
PLANNING PROCEDURES	You will find that researching and planning a good report will take far longer than the actual writing of it. Once you have gathered information from at least two sources, group related ideas together on separate pages; this will help you determine how many sections your report will need. In what order will you deal with the information? Are you remembering to link one section to another so that the report flows well? Like a successful essay, a successful report demands to be well planned. Like an essay, a report needs to be adequately introduced and concluded, although the procedures for doing this will be different, as we shall see.
FORMAL LANGUAGE	The report should be free from any colloquialisms or abbreviations (*can't, wouldn't, it'll,* etc.). You should keep your own personality well out of the text. Nor is this the place to show off your mastery of figurative language; nevertheless, your writing should be attractively and clearly expressed in well-formed sentences which convey complex ideas and information as concisely as possible. Well-formed paragraphs arranged into logically sequenced sections are also essential if your reader is to follow the progression of your ideas comfortably.

How does a report differ from an essay?

An **essay** invites you to demonstrate your skills in presenting ideas and arguments, backed up by carefully selected evidence.

Your essay will be judged on the soundness of the structured case you present.

A **report** invites you to present research-based information accurately and concisely. It is, according to the Oxford English Dictionary, *a statement of the results of an investigation.*

Your report will be judged on the clarity and quality of the structured information you provide.

Top Tip

If you are going to the trouble to include diagrams, graphs or tables, make sure that you make it clear to the reader why they are there. Do not leave them stranded on the page. What is it that they are contributing that words alone would not?

The fact that in a report it is your *information* rather than your *case* which is under the microscope allows you a certain flexibility in presenting your material. While your report should of course be written in formal prose, you are allowed to introduce any presentation techniques that you feel may make information more comprehensible and accessible to the reader. These may include:

- diagrams
- pie-charts/graphs/tables
- bullet points
- numbered sub-headings.

Making a start

Establishing a focus

It is essential that you agree with your teacher the exact focus of your report. For Intermediate 2 you have a limit of 1000 words; for Higher you have 1300. This means that you must choose your topic carefully. Avoid too broad a sweep. A report on the effects of mobile phones on society would probably be unmanageable here, but an overview of how mobile phones are seen to be affecting health might be more realistic. Consider, too, how easy or difficult you think it would be to collect the necessary information. Some basic research at an early stage might help you determine the feasibility of the task you intend setting yourself.

Establishing the audience

Once you have decided your focus, you need then to decide for whom your report is intended. How much do they already know? How technical can you allow yourself to be? This is probably a decision best taken in conjunction with your teacher, but a sensible approach might be to target the general reader. Should this be your intention then you must take care to avoid becoming overly technical in your expression or overloading them with statistics which are meaningless without suitable explanations. Some audiences, however, may already possess some topic knowledge, so you must be careful not to talk down to your reader. Teachers and parents, for instance, will be familiar with certain aspects of some school-related subjects.

Gathering information

Once you have some idea of the task you are setting yourself, you need to determine an action plan for the next stage.

- What information do you need?
- Where are you going to look for it?
- How easy is it going to be to find it?
- How much information do you need?

This, you will find, is perhaps the most critical point in determining the success or otherwise of your report. You may be setting yourself an impossible task. The information you are seeking may not exist in a format you can easily access or fully understand. You may need to re-think your topic at this stage. Although it may be dispiriting to do so, it is much better to change your task at this stage than try to soldier on with inadequate source material or material with which you are not comfortable. But does the information you *are* coming across suggest some related topic?

Top Tip

To ensure you are not guilty of inadvertent plagiarism, always make sure your notes from sources are made in your own words. If you do copy down extracts from your source, highlight them in colour to remind yourself that work is required to paraphrase the information before you use it.

Top Tip

Before you commit yourself fully to an idea for a report, do a quick search for source material. If this is not readily forthcoming, what are you finding out about? Could *this* form the basis of a report? Be flexible on choice of topic at this stage.

Seeking out sources

Where you go looking for your sources will depend entirely on the subject of your report.

If it is one of the hot topics of the day, one which appears regularly on our television screens or in our newspapers, then the archives of a quality newspaper or news magazine may be a useful starting point. Has there been a government statement/report on the topic? Have MPs had their say in parliament? Has there been a think tank study of it? If the subject concerns a commercial company in some way, has their public relations department issued press releases? Is there any academic/university comment available? Carefully worded queries along these lines in a search engine may produce useful results.

If your topic is less immediately topical, you may find your library catalogue will bring you the results you require. Consulting your school or college librarian would be a useful step if you are having a problem finding evidence. Do not overlook the usefulness of a questionnaire about your topic to your own contacts.

Surveys, databases, radio/tv interviews, letters to newspapers, personal testimony: all are possible sources depending on the angle of your enquiry. But remember, whatever information you glean, you will need to paraphrase it into your own words; a report is no place for quotations. *You* are responsible for the information you are conveying; it is *your* expression of this information which is being assessed.

Evaluating your information

In our multimedia age when information is readily available, make sure your information/statistics are the most recent possible. Of course, if there were, say, a report issued in 2002 and another in 2010, you may wish to make a useful point about how advances have been made in understanding in the interim.

Check also for any obvious commercial bias if you are using a website – .org or .ac.uk tend to be more independent information sources than .com. Be careful, too, with .gov: governments have axes to grind in the same way as commercial companies. Does your source have sufficient standing to impress an impartial reader? Sources need to be authoritative if your report is to carry weight.

Organising your information

Once you have acquired what you consider to be an appropriate quantity of information, set about organising it into categories. These may be for and against and neutral, the views of the general public/politicians/academics, international versus British public opinion, opinion from medical/press/religious sources, etc. The number of voices you wish to feature on the issue in question could give you the number of sections in the body of your report.

Structuring your report

In a real-world situation, reports are written to be read by busy people who may not have the time to re-read them. The information, therefore, has to be easily assimilated, laying emphasis on the need not just for clarity of expression but for logically organised structure.

Flow of information is vital in a successful report.

This may take the form of verbal linkage from one topic to the next: *But while the commercial world may be unanimous in its confidence in mobile phones, the medical profession seems much less so.*

Flow is also helped by numbered or titled sub-headings. Here is how a report on mobile phones and health *might* be laid out. These headings and numberings could vary according to the nature of your own topic; what is essential is that your layout should make your information clearly and instantly accessible.

Note that 1.1 makes clear the *purpose* of the report and 1.2 makes clear what procedures were followed to gather the information. These are important features of a successful introduction.

1. Introduction

For some time now, mobile phones have been a feature of daily life in the developed world. Since 1990 we have seen a rapid growth in their usage by ... This usage, however, has not come without its concerns ... These concerns were first voiced by ...

1.1 *The purpose of this report is to give an overview of informed opinion regarding the effects of mobile phone usage on public health. It will examine how ...*

1.2 *The sources consulted to arrive at these findings reflect a cross-section of recent commentators from the worlds of ...*

2. Findings

The earliest concerns were raised in ... by ... who noted that ...

2.1 *The communications industry has remained resolutely convinced of the safety of its product, going as far as to ...*

2.2 *The medical world is by no means unanimous in its opinion. A BMA report in ... suggested that ...*

2.3 *Consumer groups have shown considerable scepticism towards some of the industry's findings, claiming that ...*

2.4 *The British Government, for its part, has recently commissioned a report in an attempt to ...*

3. Discussion

It can be seen from the above information that there is a fair degree of dissent between the industry and its critics. Perhaps understandably, the industry has repeatedly defended itself and its product, maintaining that ... Their critics are by no means unanimous with medical opinion split between ... Given also the fact that symptoms may take decades to appear, it is perhaps too early to ...

4. Conclusion

While there is as yet no unanimity of opinion as to the absolute safety of these devices, the most recent independent research would appear to indicate that ... Added to this is the fact that ...

On balance then, it would seem that ... provided that ...

Presenting your report

A good report is not just one which is well-researched, well-organised and well-written, it is one whose very appearance carries authority.

Its appearance needs to reflect the same kind of professionalism expected in the commercial or academic world. Here are a few pointers to consider before your final draft.

- Include a title page. The title of your report, your name and the date of presentation on a separate page creates a certain impressive formality.
- Double-space your text and leave wide margins. Above all, do not cram text onto the page.
- Headings and sub-headings should be emphasised in some way – in bold or underlined.
- If you have used charts or tables, they should be numbered and captioned, with care taken to express exactly what they are.
- Paragraphs should be concise and well-focused. A strong, general statement should form the opening sentence of each, followed by supporting evidence. Together, they form what constitutes each section of your findings. The evidence, however, has to be paraphrased into your own words.
- A bibliography of the sources consulted should round-off the professional presentation of your research. This, like the title page, will look best occupying a separate sheet.

Bibliographical referencing

There are various ways of constructing a bibliography. These ways are referred to as 'documentation styles'. Your teacher may have a view on which one of these documentation styles is preferable in this case. Once you have decided on a documentation style, be careful to stick consistently to its procedures.

The following examples are how research sources should be laid out according to APA documentation style (American Psychological Association), a popular documentation style in schools and universities.

Make sure that your sources appear in the bibliography in alphabetical order according to the surname of the author. You will see how to lay out the author's name and what elements of the publication need to be mentioned. Once you have given the author's name (set out as below), give the date of publication, the name of the publication, the place of publication and finally the name of the publisher. Be careful to respect the *punctuation* of these layouts.

Top Tip

Nothing looks shoddier than a bibliography in which documentation style is not applied consistently. Don't let down your report with poorly presented bibliographic work.

Books

King, R. (2000) *Brunelleschi's Dome.* London: Penguin.

Newspapers and magazines

Goring, R. (2003, January 4) She's Talking Our Language Now. *The Herald,* p.14.

Reference works with no named author

Chambers Biographical Dictionary. (1984). Edinburgh: Chambers.

Government/organisation report

Department for Education and Employment. (2001). *Schools: Building on Success.* London: The Stationery Office.

Electronically sourced material

Name and title of article/publication as you would for a print publication, but instead of the place of publication and the name of the publisher, put the web address, the date the text was posted (if available) and the date you accessed it.

If you need further help on documentation style, consult http://www.docstyles.com/apacrib.htm

How does all this look in practice?

Here is part of a report on the future wind power industry in Scotland. In the findings section (2), the writer has already considered the effect on the environment (2.1), popular reaction (2.2) and cost (2.3).

Here he is examining the reliability argument with regard to wind power.

2.4 How reliable is wind power?

A statement section (note more than one sentence) which sets out the topic for discussion in the upcoming paragraph indicating that the forthcoming evidence will not be unanimous.

For years wind power, along with solar and wave power, has been seen as central to the nucleus of power sources that are a byword for sustainability. Whereas fossil fuels such as oil and coal have a finite life, wind power has long been seen as a permanent fixture in our climatic environment. (FAO 1990) Recently, however, doubts have been raised, not as to its permanence, but rather as to its reliability as a power source.

Evidence source, detailing negative side of the reliability debate.

Analysing data from the Balancing Mechanism Reporting System of the National Grid, the Caithness Wind Information Forum found that in the first five months of 2010 wind turbines from Scotland's 1588 wind farms operated at just over half of their expected maximum installed capacity, producing 17% of that capacity rather than 30%. For 80% of the time between February and June, they were operating at less than 30%. For nearly a third of this period they operated at only 5% of their maximum output. Such data has prompted the John Muir Trust, which campaigns to protect Scotland's wildernesses, to question the alleged security of supply of power from this source and raise concerns as to the wisdom of becoming more reliant on wind power, blaming vested interests for overhasty belief in this source's reliability.

Another authoritative voice questioning the reliability of wind power.

Evidence cited to refute earlier claims, setting out reliability issue more positively.

Balancing this view was that of a spokesperson for Scottish Renewables, the trade body of the energy industry, who noted that production trends have to be looked at over a longer time period and that the most recent annual figure revealed that over a fifth of Scotland's electricity was produced from renewable sources (although no figure was given for the percentage of wind power in this total). The UK government appears to share this view, commenting in the same newspaper article (Fyall 2010) that wind speeds have been lower than the nine-year average in each of the first five months of this year. According to the same government source, it is claimed that the likelihood of low wind speeds affecting 50% of the country happens less than 100 hours every year. Views on the reliability of this seemingly sustainable source are clearly not as unanimous as might previously have been thought; this will be explored further in the discussion section of this report.

> Further evidence in support of reliability of wind power.

The report should be derived from at least two sources. Here we see how one source, a newspaper article by Jenny Fyall in Scotland on Sunday, published on the 18 July 2010, has produced a rich seam of information. The report writer here has used the remarks of only four commentators, but there were others in the article which could also have been cited. Note how the writer has avoided any evaluation himself, concentrating on citing evidence of division of opinion. His only comment is that the evidence is not unanimous. In the final sentence, however, he indicates that there will be some discussion of the implications of these facts in the next section.

(FAO 1990) A reference to a report by the Food and Agricultural Organisation of the United Nations which was published in 1990 and backs up previous remarks. The report's details would need to be set out in a bibliography. (See previous section on how to lay out information from an organisation report.)

(Fyall 2010) Reference in text to the newspaper article from which all this information on wind power in Scotland comes. Used like this, the reference will need to be laid out fully in your bibliography. (See previous section for how to lay out reference to a newspaper article.)

Alternative approaches to report writing

Much of what has been suggested about report writing here relates to how reports might be approached in the academic world. The guidelines set out here will be useful if you continue this form of writing at college or university. Remember, however, that if you enter the world of commerce and business, you would find that the individual companies probably have their own agreed ways of setting out reports. Nevertheless, what you learned here about formal, detached prose writing will stand you in good stead. In government circles, too, report writing uses similar uncommitted language but makes considerable use of bullet points, tables and charts. The Scottish Government website is a mine of useful models for this approach to reports.

Consult with your teacher to see which approach would be the most appropriate one for you to use in your particular report.

Top Tip

To see how the official world sets out reports, go to www.scotland. gov.uk/publications and scroll down their list of reports. Many are fairly short and provide useful insight to how officialdom approaches report writing. Would this approach suit your topic?

Personal reflective essay

Stepping up your skills

This is a genre with which you are familiar from your work in Standard Grade or Intermediate 1. Many candidates find this an enjoyable form of writing since there is no subject we know more about than our own lives and experiences. You are the world expert on yourself, your family and friends, so this should give you the confidence to write well.

But be careful. There are critical points to watch out for. You have left Standard Grade or Intermediate 1 behind you, so your Higher/Intermediate 2 writing folio needs to demonstrate a real step-up in your writing skills. The examiner will be looking for even greater competence in producing:

- content that is sufficiently substantial to allow real depth of thought and reflection;
- structure that leads the reader convin cingly and satisfyingly through your experience;
- expression and vocabulary that fully bring alive your experience, with sentence structure which shows real variety and skill in construction;
- technical accuracy which reveals mastery of spelling, grammar and punctuation.

Let's look at these points in more detail.

Content

Choose your experience wisely. Your first descent down the flume in a Florida water park is going to be rather limited in scope for reflection. On the other hand, your first brush with American lifestyles and culture could bear profitable inspection. Your feelings, reactions and reflections on this are as important as the events themselves. If you end up with merely a catalogue of incidents, there is clearly something missing from your essay.

Structure

Planning is essential to shape your essay in a way that the reader finds easy and interesting to follow. Personal though the experience it describes may be, your essay needs to follow a structure as rigorous as an essay on a Shakespeare play or the benefits of renewable energies. You will need to introduce your topic in a way that hooks the reader; you will also have to set out and develop various aspects of the experience in a number of coherently linked paragraphs. Finally, you should stand back from your experience to reflect on its significance for you.

Expression

You spent considerable time in earlier years (and are currently doing the same in Higher/ Intermediate 2) commenting on other writers' expression and word choice. Now it is time for you to put into practice the skills you have noted at work in their writing. You have discussed how word choice is effective in creating a certain atmosphere, how onomatopoeia conjures up sounds of an experience, how a list can be used to create special effects, so now it is your turn. You should yourself employ all the techniques you noted in other writers' work. Show yourself to be a worthy member of the writers' club!

Technical accuracy

You are not under exam pressure to produce this essay; you have the time afforded by the drafting process to help you organise your ideas to their best advantage. This means you have the time to check and edit all aspects of the writing process; inaccurate spelling, grammar and punctuation should not be allowed to let down your good ideas.

Putting it all together

Here is how writer Leslie Thomas recreates for the reader an incident from his teenage years in a way which not only brings alive the event itself but describes the emotions it aroused and the significance it took on for him. It is a description of a swimming race in which he took part.

On the day a fine crowd was banked high alongside the pool, full of summer enthusiasm and summer colour. There were dozens of boys in the under fifteen races, but only myself and one other youth in the over fifteen event. He was eighteen, muscled, bronzed and lithe, and I stood beside him on the edge of the bath, skinny, with my costume hanging around my middle like a droopy loin cloth.

We bent on the starting edge, the pistol cracked, we dived, and my trunks came down, all in a matter of seconds. It might seem funny now, but then it was a moment of awful horror and shame, with everyone screaming with laughter as though I were the clown of the show. Somehow I pulled the trunks up around my bum and crying tears of anger and rage at my own stupidity I set out after my only rival who was nearly home. He beat me by thirty yards out of fifty, and I staggered from the bath, glad that my face was wet anyway so they wouldn't see I was crying. They were still laughing, a lot of them, but I called them bleeding swines under my breath and I went up to the rostrum to receive my prize for coming second.

The Tarzan youth had been presented with a pigskin hairbrush and comb. I got a hairbrush without a comb, which I bore proudly and happily to my uncle, and kept on the window ledge behind my bed when I returned to Dickies.

(From *This Time Next Week*, Leslie Thomas. Constable 1991)

Clearly, this extract is not an essay in itself but it epitomises the kind of writing you should be targeting. It captures in a lively way what it was like to be there on that summer day, but it also records the various feelings and reactions of the writer, not just then but now, as he thinks back. So how does he achieve all this? Let's take a look at how the experience is brought alive by using many of the techniques with which you are already familiar from Standard Grade. Note, too, the description of the conflicting emotions felt by Leslie Thomas, which are essential here if the episode is to be given significance.

'a fine crowd was banked high alongside the pool, full of summer enthusiasm and summer colour.'	The crowd was 'banked high' and it was 'full of summer enthusiasm and summer colour'. The *word choice* and *repetition* underlines the exact placing of the crowd and the kind of noise and colour that surrounded the pool.
'He was eighteen, muscled, bronzed and lithe ... I [was] skinny, with my costume hanging round my middle like a droopy loin cloth.'	Here we have *contrast* with the *list* of the other competitor's strengths and the writer's appearance which ends in a humorous *simile*.
'We bent ..., the pistol cracked, we dived, and my trunks came down ...'	Note a second *list* of actions with the final item giving an *anti-climax* to the list.
'crying tears of anger and rage ... glad that my face was wet anyway so they wouldn't see I was crying.'	Despite the humour of the description, there is emotion being described, too. This is necessary to give meaning to the incident. This is as important as the event itself. Make sure you are equally alert to your feelings when you are writing.
'It might seem funny now, but then it was a moment of awful horror and shame ...'	Notice how the perspective of time has changed the way he views the experience *now*.
'which I bore happily and proudly to my uncle ...'	The emotions change over the course of the incident. These are fully captured. Be alert to similar swings of mood in your own writing.

So before you embark on a personal reflective essay:

- Think back over the techniques you learned for close reading in earlier years. Use them where they are useful. Draw, too, on autobiographies you may have enjoyed reading. How did these authors deal with incidents from their past?
- Make a note, too, of the importance of self-awareness. Incidents without reflection lose much of their interest.
- Check your feelings today about the incidents you describe. Compare them with what you remember feeling at the time.

Top Tip

This type of essay is called personal reflective writing. Make sure it is as reflective as it is personal! Performing only one half of the task would seriously diminish your chances of success.

So what shall I write about?

There is probably nothing more alarming than being told you can write about anything you choose in your life. Suddenly, your mind goes blank. To help you decide what it is you are going to focus on, here are just some suggestions to locate ways forward. Often the line between all of these will become blurred as you write about them, but thinking under these headings may help you get started.

Event-driven experience: a happy/ disastrous holiday; a family landmark such as a christening, a wedding, a funeral, a divorce, moving house; a memorable journey; a sporting/musical/acting event in which you were successful/ unsuccessful; a time when you got lost or you lost something/ someone precious to you; a serious illness experienced by you or someone close to you.

Emotion-driven experience: often these will be connected to events themselves but perhaps it is the emotion you felt that initially triggers the memory. A time when you first experienced real anger, fear, shame, isolation, responsibility, prejudice, disappointment or even jealousy would be well worth exploring. So also would be feelings triggered by looking at a photograph that brings back memories or listening to a piece of music which does the same.

Relationship-driven experience: changes in family relationships brought about by growing up; an alteration in a friendship/acquaintanceship either for the better or the worse; how you felt let down by a relationship you thought you could count on.

Activity-driven experience: your interest in a particular sporting, musical, social, political or literary activity and its effects on your life/personality could produce rich results. Perhaps you are interested in amateur dramatics, performing in musicals, cooking; all these are well worth exploring in personal reflective writing.

Event-driven experience → Me ← Emotion-driven experience
Activity-driven experience → Me ←
Relationship-driven experience ↑ Me

Top Tip

Only deal with an experience/event you know or remember really well. If you write about what actually happened and your response to it, this will come through convincingly. Markers are quick to spot invention.

Planning effectively

In the Leslie Thomas extract, we saw how the experience was recreated for us by the author's use of detail; we learned about the weather, the crowd, the race, his opponent, his feelings before, during and after the race. The detail made the experience seem alive; we felt we were actually there. It had a ring of truth about it. It is that ring of truth you need to capture in your own writing. Brainstorm your ideas in a mind map or spider diagram before setting about organising the results. In planning your essay include detail at every level in a series of steps.

Step 1. Jot down the actual events to be covered in the essay; how the day/event/experience started; the day/event/experience itself; the end of the day/event/experience. In this way, you will remind yourself of the overall factual content which needs to be included. This will give you a rough idea of the number of body paragraphs in the essay.

Step 2. List the detail you might include to bring alive the content. What was the weather like that day? How were your family behaving towards you? Was there a journey involved? What was it like? How did you travel? Were you on your own? Were you with people? How were they behaving? Did they share your reactions to what was happening? Where was all this taking place? Describe your surroundings. Was your sense of smell, touch, hearing or taste involved at any time?

Step 3. Explore your feelings at various points of the experience. What were you feeling when you woke up that day? Did the weather seem to match your mood? Did your feelings change over the course of events? Did you feel increasingly nervous/confident/bored/frightened? Was there a sudden mood swing?

Step 4. Reflect on the experience. You now have the benefit of hindsight as you look back on this moment in your life. Are your feelings about this experience the same as they were then, or has growing up altered the way you view that experience? How do you view yourself as you look back on the person you were then? Proud? Ashamed? Amazed at how you have changed? How do you look on the people involved in this experience? More tolerant of their behaviour? More critical?

> **Top Tip**
>
> Always break down an experience into smaller sections and try to remember the details of fact and feeling you noticed at the time. Details convince; generalisations don't.

Quick Task

With a partner, discuss how well or badly the following extracts perform the task of bringing experience/personality/reactions to life. Say exactly what is wrong with the extracts you find weak; pick out what make the better ones convincing.

a) *We got up when mum woke us and before long we were on our way.*

b) *My sister always maintains I have a chip on my shoulder and for a long time I denied this, laughing off her comments as fanciful. But one day last spring it was brought home to me very powerfully that perhaps she had a point. It happened like this.*

c) *Rain had spat at the window all night. The relentless downpour matched my gloomy mood as I lay awake contemplating what lay ahead of me the next day. By four o'clock I eventually managed to fall into a fitful doze. Hardly surprisingly, therefore, my mood was not of the best when the jeering ring of my alarm clock jolted me awake at six.*

d) *I looked around me at this great arena. Everywhere I looked there were people. This was one of the biggest places I had ever competed. Soon we got started and my nerves gradually settled down.*

e) *The perfume of lilies was heavy in the air. Guests whispered among themselves as the organist indulged in some holy doodling. Sweet papers rustled. Mothers shooshed restless children. Time passed. But only slowly. The bride was late. Very late. I was beginning to feel ever so slightly nervous.*

f) *I had not been all that keen on my dad marrying again but Sheena was okay. I liked her and she was a good laugh. We all thought so except my sister. She said she missed my mum.*

g) *I was sad to leave our old house but once we were in the car I started to think about our new house. Soon we were in Perth and eventually we arrived at where we were to stay the night. I shared a room with my sister in the hotel. We stayed up and watched tv until really late. It was great.*

h) *The arena towered over us all, making the capacity crowd look like so many ants huddled together for warmth. Smithy appeared even more nervous than me; his skinny knees were actually shaking. Not a pretty sight. Armstrong, of course, appeared to be taking it all in his stride. Come on, I shouted silently to myself. Let's get this show on the road.*

Quick Task

Personal reflective writing is all about using your own experiences. So try this. You woke up only a few hours ago. Write a paragraph of detailed sentences about your experiences from the point of waking up to getting to school or college, applying the detail-focused approach we have been examining.

Getting started

Although writing a personal reflective essay may not involve you in the kind of research you needed for a persuasive/argumentative essay, you need to be just as alert to the structuring of your essay as you were in putting forward ideas and opinions.

INTRODUCTION	You need to capture the reader's attention with the first sentence. The first sentence is probably even more important here than in discursive writing since an important aim of this kind of writing is to give pleasure as well as information to the reader. Even if you are writing about a sad event, you need to offer a rich reading experience. This opening hook can take various forms as we shall see shortly. The background to what is to follow should also be clearly set out so that the reader is prepared for what you have to offer in the body paragraphs.
BODY PARAGRAPHS	A strong statement at the beginning of each paragraph will help focus your ideas on the various aspects of the experience you are going to explore in the rest of the paragraph. A reflective comment somewhere in each paragraph would also be helpful for the reader in understanding the significance you are placing on the experience.
CONCLUSION	Here is where you stand well back from the events and experiences you have been describing. You have the advantage of time now and you can compare your present feelings with what you felt at the time. The broader the gap between the two, the greater your maturity may seem to have developed. Examiners lap this up!

The introduction

In this type of writing you have great freedom of approach. There is no one way to set about hooking your reader; the essential thing is that the reader gets hooked. Here are two practical ways to start.

The chronological start

With this approach you tackle your material in chronological order and build up the experience as it evolves.

> It was a Tuesday when the letter arrived. I had been expecting it for some time, of course, but seeing it lying there with the initials of the national kayaking association on the envelope made me gulp. Had I been chosen to represent Great Britain in Germany? Holding it as if it were red hot, I sidled into the kitchen where my mum was mopping up the mess round the dog's bowl. Turning and seeing the envelope, she raised her eyes questioningly. 'For heaven's sake, open it then,' she pleaded, her voice jumping an octave in her excitement. 'Are you in?'
>
> Indeed I was. So four weeks later I found myself at Glasgow airport waiting for British Airways flight BA 422 bound for Berlin.

Starting at the beginning and working your way through material does not need to be boring. The first sentence is totally factual but it hooks the reader efficiently. What was in the letter? We want to know. Notice, too, that information we need to know to make sense of the rest of the essay is carefully planted: this is the essay by someone who kayaks rather well and might be in the running to represent her country at international level. There is plenty of detail here to bring the scene in the kitchen alive; we are interested in this person's situation. Notice, too, how the next paragraph is linked subtly to the last by a question-and-answer structure. The essay is now up and running.

The flash-forward start

Have you ever noticed that good films often start in the middle of something quite exciting, leaving you to wait for an explanation of what is going on? The film usually then moves backwards in time to give you the necessary information for a fuller understanding. This technique works well in personal reflective writing, too.

Top Tip

The openings of some 'first person' short stories have much in common with the starts of good personal reflective essays. Try to find some; they may give you ideas about different approaches to launching your essay.

> It was the lights I was most aware of. Mercilessly, they shone into my face, leaving the building behind them a darkened, gloomy shell. They were hot, too, the lights. I could feel sweat starting to pour down my face. My hair was already sticking to my brow. I walked forward confidently. I might be scared but there was no way 'they' were going to see it. It was up to me now. I sat down on the seat they indicated. Black and white shimmered beneath my sweat-filled eyes. Sonata in C sharp minor here we come.
>
> Let me say right away that I had never wanted to take part in the Arbroath Competitive Music Festival but it's amazing what pushy parents can do to you. I had started playing the piano when I was six and really enjoyed it but at the time I seemed pretty average.

So what is going on here, you wonder in the first couple of sentences. But you are hooked. Is it a Nazi-type interrogation? No, it's someone preparing to play in a piano competition. Only gradually is this made apparent and the writer finally jumps back in time to explain exactly what is going on.

There are as many ways of opening a personal reflective essay as there are stories to tell. So feel free to experiment.

The body paragraphs

When you are planning your essay, you should give thought to the number and content of your body paragraphs. What is each one going to focus on? A strong, clear statement of intent at the start of each one will help to give shape to your thoughts for the rest of the paragraph. It will also help the reader focus on what is to come. Don't be afraid either to offer a comment on what you are feeling in each one.

The conclusion

This is where a candidate can really impress the reader/examiner. This is your chance to make clear you have reflected fully on what has been happening to you. Indeed, if you are writing about something in your earlier life, you can offer two perspectives: one summing up your feelings at the time of the events/experience; the other coloured by the distance of time as you consider yourself and your responses then. How has your judgement of events and of yourself changed? Here are some useful phrases to launch such reflections:

Top Tip

Conclusions in personal reflective writing are where you bare your feelings for inspection. Show yourself to be a thoughtful person, fully aware of your weaknesses but also of your strengths; some-one who has not only *lived through* the events but *thought through* them as well.

> Of course I see now that ... was only doing his best. How could he possibly have known that ... As I look back I blush a bit, but that was how it felt then when ... Since then I feel I have become much more ...
>
> Yes, I suppose I was behaving ... But I was only nine after all. Now, I see that ...
>
> That was then. Now, my feelings about her are rather more ... I can barely recognise the person who ...
>
> With the perspective of time, I see matters rather differently. Then I was ... Now I hope I am a little more ...
>
> With the benefit of hindsight, there is no doubt that I was in the wrong. Had I thought about it a bit more I would have seen that ... Still, we can all be wise after the event. What is important now is that ...

How am I coming across?

By its nature, this is a very personal kind of writing. Sometimes we can become too close to our work to be able to judge it objectively.

Before finalising your essay, ask yourself:

Is my narrative clear? Or is there something which doesn't quite make sense to a reader who doesn't know the background?
Is there anything that needs to be added?
Is the balance between narrative and reflection correct?
Is my expression clear? Or are there some sentences which need to be read twice to be understood?
Have I managed to include elements of style such as metaphors, similes, personification?
How does my personality come across to the reader? Does the person I am writing about seem likeable?
Is this the personality I thought I was projecting?
Will reading this essay help the reader understand me better?
More importantly, has writing this essay helped ME understand myself better?

Editing your text

No, this is not the boring part of the folio process! It's the part where you can maybe make the difference between one grade and a better one.

You will be amazed how many slips may have crept in as you have been adding and deleting words, sentences and paragraphs in your various drafts.

Check your strategy

- Make sure you have enough time in your schedule to let some time pass between writing what you think may be your final draft and editing it. Coming fresh to it will perhaps reveal mistakes you overlooked previously.
- Read the essays ALOUD to yourself. Does the text read well? Reading aloud will identify the clumsy sentence or missing word. (The chances are that if you read the essay over in your head, you will pass over mistakes or omissions time and time again and fail to notice them.) Have you any sentences which seem overlong? Break them down into shorter units. Are there some sentences which might do better combined? Examine one sentence at a time to make sure it is as polished as it might be.
- Will the examiner be able to follow the line of your arguments in discursive work? Have you included sufficient connectives to make the sentences and sections flow into each other? Or does your text read like a list? See 'Linking words and phrases' on page 82 of this *Success Guide*.
- Is there structure to your paragraphs, whatever the genre? Are there any comments that might confuse the reader here and would do better elsewhere or in a paragraph of their own? In discursive pieces, are your introduction and conclusion fulfilling their function convincingly?
- Does your chosen style SOUND convincing throughout for what you are trying to do? Or have you made some errors with word choice in places, words which are perhaps too chatty or too formal for their context?
- Talking of words, are they all your own? Have you checked for accidental plagiarism in discursive pieces? Go back carefully over sections where you have used research.
- Check with your teacher's comments. Have you taken previous feedback fully into account?

Check your tactics

- Make sure you have laid out the text in a way that looks impressive. Examiners are only human and an attractively presented text cannot help but make a good initial impression. Folio pieces can be typed, word-processed or neatly handwritten, although the SQA encourages that submissions be word-processed. Only one side of the page should be used. Further SQA recommendations are as follows:

Keep to a standard font, e.g. Times New Roman, Ariel, Calibri
Point size should be 12
Alignment should be left or justified
Allow 2 cm all round for margins
Line spacing should be 1·5 or 2
Print colour: black (except possibly graphs, diagrams, etc. in a report)

- Perhaps you will wish to alter type size for headings if you are tackling a report, but do so consistently. If you have used a numbering system, check that they are in numerical sequence – adding and deleting text on a computer can easily upset this.
- Don't forget to include the essay title at the top of the page; if you have produced a report or a script, a separate title page will look professional.
- If you have included a bibliography, make sure you have laid it out strictly – and consistently – according to the documentation style of your choice. See the report section of this *Success Guide* to double-check.
- Check also for missing punctuation, particularly if you used direct speech in a short story, personal reflective essay or monologue.
- In longer sentences where the subject may be at some distance from the verb, check that a singular subject has not accidentally ended up with a plural verb, or vice versa.
- The spell check on your computer is not foolproof: yes, it will help with 'accommodation' and 'separate' but it will not help if you have typed 'bit' instead of 'but'. Look doubly carefully at words which have given you problems in the past.
- Double-check that the following slips are not lurking somewhere in your text; they are easily overlooked but will cause an examiner to grimace.

their/there/they're	*who's/whose*
it's/its	*were/where/we're*
too/to	

- Detail counts for a lot at this stage. You have had a full drafting process to produce your essays, so there have been adequate opportunities to identify obvious weaknesses.
- Presenting an examiner with a text containing errors which could easily have been corrected reveals a great deal about you. And what it reveals is not at all good!

Linking words and phrases

It is important for your success that you lead your reader through the text smoothly. At no point in the text should readers find themselves wondering where they are or how they got there. Throughout, there should be logical, easy-to-follow 'signposting' to ease the way forward, no matter what genre you have chosen; changes of argument in discursive essays, changes of mood in short stories, all need to be prepared for.

Connectives for discursive writing

On the following page you will find just some of the connectives and connecting phrases which will help you do this in any form of discursive writing.

These are the basic building blocks; successful usage of them will require you to make them your own. For instance, we can suggest that a phrase like *Turning from ... to ...* can help with the transition to a new topic, but how much better it would be if you were to personalise it, so to speak, with variations of your own, related to your specific topic, e.g.

Turning from the unquestionable economic benefits of ..., we are confronted with the more controversial effects of ... on the environment. Here we note that ...

Here we have signalled not simply a move from one topic to the other (financial to environmental), but from one response to another (positive to less positive).

Top Tip

Always signpost changes of direction in your text. A lost reader is potentially a hostile reader.

Listing (to enumerate sequential stages in an argument)

First(ly), ...   *Furthermore, ...*   *Finally, ...*

To begin with, ...   *Secondly, ...*   *In conclusion, ...*

In addition, ...

What is more, ...

Note:

first and foremost   }   mark the beginning of a *descending* order

first and most important(ly) }

above all   }

last but not least   }   mark the end of an *ascending* order

Transition (to lead the reader to a new stage of thought)

Now, ...

As far as ... is concerned, ...

Turning to ...

Regarding the question of ...

As for ...

Note:

Incidentally, ...   indicates a brief digression from your main topic

Contrast (with preceding comments)

(On the one hand) ... On the other hand, however, ...

By way of contrast, ...

Conversely, ...

Whereas, ...

While, ...

XXXXX, on the contrary, is ...

Concession (showing a certain surprise at what is being said given the nature of what was said before)

However, ...

Even though ....

Nevertheless, ...

Nonetheless, ...

Yet, however much we ...

XXXX notwithstanding, ...

In spite of ..., we ...

For all this, however, ...

Increase your word power

Success in Higher or Intermediate 2 English requires you to have at your disposal a vocabulary which serves you efficiently in all areas of assessment: close reading, critical essays and the writing folio all test your ability to identify and use words precisely.

It is vitally important to acquire the kind of vocabulary which will be an adequate vehicle for your ideas.

Over the years, your reading will have no doubt enriched your word power, but the following activities are geared to give your vocabulary that added boost which will mark you out as an articulate writer, one whose word skills channel your thoughts precisely and persuasively. These skills will benefit not only the extended pieces of writing for your folio but for the entire Higher and Intermediate 2 assessment process. So let's get down to it now.

Complete the sentence (1)

Choose the best ending for each of the sentence openings from the list below.

1. There is a significant variance between what the makers claim as the vehicle's petrol consumption and the reality. This **discrepancy ...**
2. Since the current king was reputed to be descended from Banquo, Shakespeare is careful to **portray ...**
3. This difference of opinion between husband and wife over a minor matter early on in the film **prefigures ...**
4. Lumsden, in his smart blazer and elegant shirts, is the very **antithesis ...**
5. While there is no doubting the depth of their feeling and outrage, their criticisms of central government are hardly **pertinent ...**
6. In her laid-back attitude to authority and responsibility, she **epitomises ...**
7. A press release featuring the poor showing of wind power in the first five months of 2010 was intended to **foreground ...**
8. Although the chairman meant well in his comments, they only served to **exacerbate ...**
9. In the line 'The child is father of the man' Wordsworth **encapsulates ...**
10. The success of the programme derives from the fact that it appeals to a wide **diversity...**

a. ... what many of the older generation consider to be the typical teenager.
b. ... him as being a strong moral character, uncorrupted like his friend by ambition.
c. ... between the two figures is not uncommon if the trade press is to be believed.
d. ... what was already a tense situation between the two warring parties.
e. ... what will occur much later in the action over a much more serious affair.
f. ... of viewers, from some of the oldest to the very young.
g. ... of his shabby colleague from Edinburgh, for whom outward appearance has little importance.

h. ... in that their problem stems from a failure in the local health service.

i . ... much of his thinking with regard to the relationship between the adult and the child.

j . ... the fact that renewable energy sources are not as reliable as was once thought.

> Now write down the word in bold and, using the context of your completed sentence, put beside it what you *think* its definition might be. Check your definition with a dictionary if you are in doubt.

Working with definitions (1)

> Below are some common items of academic vocabulary. The definitions of these words have been deliberately mixed up. Match the word on the left with its correct definition.

a. evocative	**1.** reach a final or climactic stage
b. discern	**2.** not lessened in any way
c. empathy	**3.** connected with the matter in hand
d. delineate	**4.** happening again and again
e. relevant	**5.** to consider something in its situation rather than in isolation
f. counter	**6.** bringing strong images or feelings to mind
g. recurrent	**7.** react with an opposing opinion
h. contextualise	**8.** identification with another's feelings or situation
i. unmitigated	**9.** trace the outline of something or someone
j. culminate	**10.** perceive

> Now, with the knowledge gained from matching term and definition correctly, complete the following sentences with the most appropriate term. You may need to alter the form of the word slightly to fit the sentence.

1. Time and time again in the play there is the _____ image of clothes which do not fit or belong to the owner.

2. After many years of research their efforts finally _____ in the discovery of a vaccine for polio.

3. There are many clues planted throughout the film as to the identity of the killer, some being _____, others fairly misleading.

4. Their stay in France was not an _____ success, largely because neither he nor his wife spoke French at all well.

5. Frequent use of alliteration on the letters 'k', 't' and 'r' are highly _____ of the sound of artillery.

6. Alert readers will _____ a growing hollowness in the speaker's claims to innocence.

7. Donovan is careful to _____ in some detail the spiritual as well as artistic aspects of her heroine, Fiona.

8. To critics who criticised their report for being overly long, the researchers _____ by pointing out that a topic of this enormous complexity required length to do full justice to its material.

9. It's difficult to fully appreciate the shades of meaning a word can have unless you _____ it in a longer stretch of language.

10. His basic lack of _____ with pupils makes you wonder why he sought out a career in education.

Word substitution (1)

From the list below, choose a word which could be used in place of the language in **bold** without changing the meaning of the sentence. You may need to change the form of the word and the word order in the sentence.

pragmatic	trivialise	incongruous	clarify
cathartic	stipulate	preliminary	reiterates
subtle	depicts		

1. There has been no obvious change in the government's attitude to renewable energy but experts detect a **small but significant** difference in how it refers to the issue.
2. In the second part of the report the union attempts to **explain more clearly** its reasons for arguing against any increase.
3. Although the housing schemes are to be found at opposite ends of the country, there are few differences in the way the author **writes about** them.
4. In their assessment of the savings already made, the committee is careful not to **make** the employees' efforts **seem unimportant.**
5. A **first** glance at the evidence suggests that the idea has not been properly thought through at all.
6. The second half of the essay merely **says again** what was indicated at some length in the first half.
7. There is little of high principle in their attitude to running a company; they take a view on trade which is **entirely based on how things are rather than how they should be.**
8. Since this family row had been brewing for some time, the explosion when it came was **helpful for clearing the air.**
9. There seems something **out of place** in the minute size of the grant given the enormity of the problem.
10. The bill does not give any exact date about when the increase should take effect but it does **say** that it must happen after 2012 and before 2016.

If you are in any doubt about the exact meaning of any of your substituted words, check them with a dictionary. Were you correct?

You should keep a record of the words and expressions you have learned and try to use them in essays whenever you can.

Making a critical collocation (1)

Begin by reading through the sentences below. Then select one word from the box on the left and combine it with one from the box on the right to make a critical collocation which makes a sensible combination for the gaps in each sentence.

cursory	figurative	language	anomalies
serious	adequate	development	portrayal
thematic	effective	structure	importance
paramount	logical	examination	analysis
bipartite	in-depth	sequence	response

1. The study presents us with a _____, the first part giving a summary of the system's shortcomings while the second explores possible solutions.

2. It is of _____ to understand the reasons behind the author's choice of Scots for the narrative voices if we are to understand fully her intentions.

3. To complete this _____, Rankin introduces yet a third character who is also pursued by past sins which refuse to go away.

4. An _____ of the sources for the article revealed that no less than twelve of them came from various petroleum industry websites, four from BP's PR department and three from the marketing department of Shell.

5. With little use of similes, metaphors or personification, the short story was a dull reading experience, suffering badly from this absence of _____.

6. The article with its close attention to detail offers an _____ of the life of the average university student of today.

7. Even a _____ of the disappointing figures from February to June suggests that there were clearly _____ in the earlier more positive report.

8. In the essay's arguments the reasons for change are presented in a _____, beginning with the least important before building towards the most crucial in the final section.

9. Two more officers on the beat seems hardly an _____ given the town's soaring crime figures.

- Now, attempt to put into your own words the meaning conveyed in the critical collocation of your choice.
- You will see very quickly how economical in time and words a good vocabulary is.
- You will also hear how much more articulate and authoritative effective collocations will make your essays sound.

Complete the sentence (2)

Choose the best ending for each of the sentence openings from the list below.

1. In his inability to express his feelings, Docherty's father **embodies** ...
2. Starting with the familiar genre of the crime fiction novel, Welsh manages to **transcend** it by ...
3. This is a harsh view of the city which is in **marked** contrast to that of Donovan who ...
4. By looking only at a breakdown of economic factors, the research sets itself somewhat limited **parameters**. A fuller study ...
5. The style of his writing is rather **spare** in that ...
6. Their attitude to social reform was somewhat **reminiscent** of that of aristocrats before the French Revolution in that both ...
7. Although his plans for the New Town of Edinburgh showed talent, they failed to **sustain** the interest of the buying public ...
8. She has chosen to **depict** her central character as an extraordinary auctioneer ...
9. The **exposition** of the background to the slave trade takes several chapters. This may seem lengthy ...
10. It is evidence of the report's **authority** that only six months after its publication ...

---

a. ... the government of the day had rushed through amendments to the Criminal Justice Bill.
b. ... whose strange ways and behaviour are described in convincing detail.
c. ... describes the place in far gentler, welcoming terms.
d. ... you look in vain for metaphors or similes, and only the most essential adjectives and adverbs are there.
e. ... the working class character driven to violence by the failure to find the appropriate words.
f. ... would need to look at environmental hazards and sustainability at the very least.
g. ... regarded any form of liberalism as the forerunner of social collapse.
h. ... adding a range of off-beat characters to say nothing of a probing examination of current social morality.
i. ... who gradually turned to the bolder and more imaginative ideas of younger architects.
j. ... but it is entirely necessary if we are to understand fully the many financial factors involved.

> Now, working with the understanding of the terms in bold which you have worked out here, make a list of them and put opposite each one what you think a dictionary definition of it might be. Check with a dictionary if you are still unsure.

Working with definitions (2)

Below are some common items of academic vocabulary. The definitions of these words have been deliberately mixed up. Match the word on the left with its correct definition.

a.	convey	1.	viewpoint
b.	incongruous	2.	occurring one after the other
c.	succinct	3.	exact opposite
d.	paramount	4.	communicate (an idea)
e.	antithesis	5.	not stated directly
f.	implicit	6.	more important than anything else
g.	ethos	7.	brief and clearly expressed
h.	alternate	8.	spirit/beliefs of a group/institution/place
i.	allocate	9.	lacking in harmony of scale
j.	perspective	10.	set apart for a purpose

Now, with the knowledge gained from matching term and definition correctly, complete the following sentences with the most appropriate term. You may need to alter the form of the word slightly to fit the sentence.

1. In the school he attended in his early years, the _____ was one where sporting abilities were privileged over academic ones.

2. The story is told from the _____ of three narrators.

3. On the surface, there is something distinctly _____ about one person occupying a house with twenty bedrooms.

4. When learning a foreign language it is of _____ importance to be able to use it regularly with native speakers.

5. The way the film regularly _____ between past and present leaves it open to a charge of predictability by some critics.

6. To ensure the issue is discussed impartially, each interested party is _____ exactly the same amount of words to put forward its case.

7. Being limited to a mere 140 characters ensures that every message is _____ in the extreme.

8. Although their relationship was never directly expressed there was clearly an _____ understanding between the two of them, as even a superficial reading of their correspondence indicates.

9. Efficient dialogue in a play should _____ more than information alone.

10. In her worldly desire for wealth and success, she is the _____ of her sister whose only concern is to help those less fortunate than herself.

Word substitution (2)

From the list below, choose a word which could be used in place of the language in **bold** without changing the meaning of the sentence. You may need to change the form of the word and the word order in the sentence.

vulnerable	pervasive	dichotomy
exemplify	govern	harbour (verb)
uncompromising	context	exploration
address (verb)		

1. With fog invading every part of this ruined town, there is an **all-over** atmosphere of gloom in the opening chapter of the novel.

2. Although he had various reasons to dislike his former employer, he did not **hold on to** any grudges against him.

3. With sensitive feelings like hers she is **easily wounded** and de-motivated, so sarcastic remarks like that are to be avoided.

4. Despite describing the problem for four pages, the author of the report fails to **tackle face on** the underlying causes for teenage boys' underachievement in this area.

5. Quoting these remarks will not impress the examiner unless you can indicate the **situation where this remark came from** in the text.

6. There is often a **difference** between what he intends to do and what he actually does, the two never seeming to coincide.

7. Here is a character whose behaviour is totally **controlled** by his greed and selfishness.

8. They do not see eye to eye on this issue and her sister's attitude is such that she is **not prepared to make any allowances or exceptions** on her refusal to permit smoking in the house.

9. Any **close inspection** of the language of the text will reveal that it was written in a time before our politically correct age.

10. This is a novel which **gives a clear instance of** the writer's love of island life and culture.

If you are in any doubt about the exact meaning of any of your substituted words, check them with a dictionary. Were you correct? You should keep a record of the words and expressions you have learned and try to use them in essays whenever you can.

Making a critical collocation (2)

Begin by reading through the sentences below. Then select one word from the box on the left and combine it with one from the box on the right to make a critical collocation which gives a sensible combination for the gaps in each sentence.

evocative	comprehensive	comments	juxtaposition
explicit	discursive	description	image
incongruous	marked	stance	atmosphere
incisive	uncompromising	contrast	reference
pervasive	recurrent	exposition	approach

1. The novel begins with an _____ of a Scottish country house in the years before the First World War, capturing that moment in time powerfully.

2. While there is no _____ to increased taxation in the report, it is clear from subsequent comments that this is what they have in mind.

3. With its rapid rhythms and harsh alliteration, this second section is in _____ to the peaceful atmosphere of the opening lines.

4. Previously, he had seemed to welcome their suggestions but now he has adopted an _____, refusing fiercely to abandon his principles and give in to the promises of commercial interests.

5. He has a sharp brain and his _____ show that he has fully understood the question. Everything he says shows real insight.

6. Some commentators criticise the writer's _____, saying he takes far too long to get the narrative underway, spending too much time on landscape description and the hero's family background.

7. The seemingly _____ of a high-tech building next to a medieval one may surprise many, but stylistically it works.

8. References to bribery, intimidation and violence at all levels create a _____ of corruption.

9. He is an author who, like Shakespeare in Hamlet, enjoys exploiting the power of the _____ of an unweeded garden to suggest time and again the problems of the state.

10. As a _____ of the guiding principles of current language teaching methods, the article is invaluable.

- Now, attempt to put into your own words the meaning conveyed in the critical collocation of your choice. You will see very quickly how economical in time and words a good vocabulary is.
- List any other sensible combination of the above words you notice. Note how effective collocations make you sound highly articulate and how they add authority to your comments.
- Start adopting them in your essays now!

Answers

Complete the sentence (1)

1. C
2. B
3. E
4. G
5. H
6. A
7. J
8. D
9. I
10. F

Working with definitions (1)

A 6
B 10
C 8
D 9
E 3
F 7
G 4
H 5
I 2
J 1

1. recurrent
2. culminated
3. relevant
4. unmitigated
5. evocative
6. discern
7. delineate
8. countered
9. contextualise
10. empathy

Word substitution (1)

1. subtle
2. clarify
3. depicts
4. trivialise
5. preliminary
6. reiterates
7. pragmatic
8. cathartic
9. incongruous
10. stipulate

Making a critical collocation (1)

1. bipartite structure
2. paramount importance
3. thematic development
4. in-depth analysis
5. figurative language
6. effective portrayal
7. cursory examination/serious anomalies
8. logical sequence
9. adequate response

Complete the sentence (2)

1. C
2. B
3. E
4. G
5. H
6. A
7. J
8. D
9. I
10. F

Working with definitions (2)

A 4
B 9
C 7
D 6
E 3
F 5
G 8
H 2
I 10
J 1

1. ethos
2. perspective
3. incongruous
4. paramount
5. alternates
6. allocated
7. succinct
8. implicit
9. convey
10. antithesis

Word substitution (2)

1. pervasive
2. harbour
3. vulnerable
4. address
5. context
6. dichotomy
7. governed
8. uncompromising
9. exploration
10. exemplifies

Making a critical collocation (2)

1. evocative description
2. explicit reference
3. marked contrast
4. uncompromising stance
5. incisive comments
6. discursive approach
7. incongruous juxtaposition
8. pervasive atmosphere
9. recurrent image
10. comprehensive exposition

Acknowledgments

Leckie & Leckie is grateful to the copyright holders, as credited, for permission to use their material:

- Garnethill. Denise Mina (1998), p. 14.
- Hieroglyphics and other stories. Anne Donovan. Canongate Books Ltd (2001), p. 16.
- 'Napoleon and I' in Selected Stories. Ian Crichton Smith. Carcanet Press (1990), p. 20.
- 'All The Little Loved Ones' in Red Tides. Dilys Rose (1993), p. 20.
- 'A Deep Hole' in Beggars Banquet. Ian Rankin. Orion (2002), p. 20.
- 'Hieroglyphics' in Hieroglyphics and other stories. Anne Donovan. Canongate (2001), p. 20.
- 'A story of folding and unfolding' in Free Love and other stories. Ali Smith. Virago, an imprint of Little Brown Book Group (1995), p. 21.
- 'The Black Devon' orginally published in In the Event of Fire. ASLS. Corinne Fowler (2009), p. 21.
- 'The Only Only' in New Writing 3. Candia McWilliams. Gillon Aitken Associates/Minerva (1994), p. 21.
- 'A House in Sicily' in The Penguin Book of Scottish Short Stories. Neil McCallum. Penguin (1970), p. 21.
- Between Man and Woman Keys' in Three Kinds of Kissing. Rosalind Brackenbury (1993), p. 21.
- 'Paris' in The Devil and the Giro. Ronald Frame. Canongate Books Ltd (1989), p. 22.
- 'South America' in Secret Villages. Douglas Dunn. Faber and Faber (1985), p. 22.
- 'Her Mother's Songs' originally published in The Dynamics of Balsa. ASLS. Merryn Glover (2007), p. 22.
- 'College' in Free Love and other stories. Ali Smith. Virago, an imprint of Little Brown Book Group (1995), p. 22.
- 'Fallers' originally published in The Dynamics of Balsa. ASLS. Andy Manders (2007), p. 22.
- 'A Good Night's Sleep' in Under Cover. Brian McCabe. Mainstream Publishing (1993), p. 22.
- 'Glasgow Sonnet No. 1' in Collected Poems. Edwin Morgan. Carcanet Press (1990), p. 30.
- The Blues' in This Folding Map. Alan Riach. Auckland University Press (1991), p. 32.
- Prospecting in Partick' orginally published in The Event of Fire: New Writing Scotland 27. ASLS. Valerie Thorton (2009), p. 34.
- Timetable' in Slattern. Kate Clanchy. Picador/Macmillan (1995), p. 35.
- 'Seagull' in Body Parts. Brian McCabe. Canongate Books Ltd (1999). P. 35.
- Bold Girls. Rona Munro. Hodder & Stoughton (1991), p. 36 and p. 39.
- The Cheviot, the Stag and the Black, Black Oil. John McGrath. Methuen Drama (1974), p. 42 and p. 43.
- Talking Heads 1. Alan Bennett. BBC Books (1988), p. 42 and p. 43.
- A scheme of mice and men best laid aside' in The Scotsman, Monday 10 May 2010. Press Association (2010), p. 48.
- From Scottish Architecture by Miles Glendinning and Aonghus MacKechnie © 2004 Thames and Hudson Ltd, London. Reprinted by kind permission of Thames and Hudson. p.52
- From This Time Next Week. Leslie Thomas. Constable (1991), p. 73.

Leckie & Leckie has made every effort to trace all copyright holders and to obtain their permission for the use of copyright material. Leckie & Leckie will gladly receive information enabling them to rectify any error or omission in subsequent editions.

Text © 2011 Dr Christopher Nicol
Design and layout © 2011 Leckie & Leckie
Cover photo and sculpture © 2008 George W. Hart, http://georgehart.com

01/060111

ISBN 978-1-84372-877-1

Published by
Leckie & Leckie
An imprint of HarperCollins*Publishers*
Westerhill Road, Bishopbriggs, Glasgow, G64 2QT
T: 0844 576 8126 F: 0844 576 8131
leckieandleckie@harpercollins.co.uk www.leckieandleckie.co.uk

Special thanks to
Planman Technologies (creative packaging and illustration),
Roda Morrison (copy-edit), Jennifer Shaw (proofread)

Leckie & Leckie makes every effort to ensure that all paper used in our books is made from wood pulp
obtained from well-managed forests, controlled sources and recycled wood or fibre.

A CIP Catalogue record for this book is available from the British Library.

Mixed Sources
Product group from well-managed
forests and other controlled sources
www.fsc.org Cert no. SW-COC-001806
© 1996 Forest Stewardship Council

FSC is a non-profit international organisation established to promote the
responsible management of the world's forests. Products carrying the FSC
label are independently certified to assure consumers that they come
from forests that are managed to meet the social, economic and
ecological needs of present and future generations.

Find out more about HarperCollins and the environment at
www.harpercollins.co.uk/green